# heartbroken,
## but not
# broken

# heartbroken,
## but not
# broken

## jaime clemmer

CFI
An imprint of Cedar Fort, Inc.
Springville, Utah

ISBN 13: 978-1-4621-4016-9

Published by CFI, an imprint of Cedar Fort, Inc.
2373 W. 700 S., Springville, UT 84663
Distributed by Cedar Fort, Inc., www.cedarfort.com

Library of Congress Control Number: 2021933618

Cover design by Courtney Proby
Cover design © 2021 by Cedar Fort, Inc.
Edited and typeset by Valene Wood

Printed in the United States of America

10 9 8 7 6 5 4 3 2 1

Printed on acid-free paper

To Jack, for his enduring love and saving me from ruin
To Finn, for his heart
To Grayson, for his courage
To Sterling, for her joy

To Sawyer's Army, for all they do to honor and remember our boy

# Contents

# Preface

*"It's important that we share our experiences with other people. Your story will heal you and your story will heal somebody else. When you tell your story, you give yourself and give other people permission to acknowledge their own story."*

—Iyanla Vanzant

I HAVE BEEN CALLED A LOT OF THINGS IN MY LIFE, BUT I HAVE NEVER been called a writer. Someone who won't stop talking, maybe. Someone who always has a story to tell, possibly. Someone who writes a lot of things down, absolutely. But I've never warranted the title of writer. Most of the titles I have been given describe a role I fill or a function I serve. All of them are in relation to others: mother, wife, PTA volunteer, boss, employee, adoptive parent, school superintendent's wife, Sunday School teacher, neighbor, friend, youth leader. The list is long. They explain the many roles I play but they do not elaborate on how I play them. I know I'm not defined by the roles assigned to me. I love my life, the roles I fill, the people I serve, and the people who serve me in those roles. But lately I have felt my roles shifting. Upon the unexpected and tragic passing of my youngest son, Sawyer, I was given a new title, one I never agreed upon, and one I tried to reject. And may I be frank? I hate it. *HATE IT.* It is the label, "Bereaved Mother."

From the moment I first set foot in the hospital right behind the ambulance, I knew I was going to write about everything surrounding this tragedy in my life, the death of my ten-year-old son Sawyer. I knew it. I was keenly aware of the ambulance driver in the ER who asked if I was "the mom." Of the tiny room an ER administrator put me in. Of the man who gave me Sawyer's socks to hold (socks that I

1

would not relinquish for days). Of the ice water they bullied me into drinking to stay hydrated and how it was so full of ice I didn't really have any water to drink. All the tiny, inconsequential details I never want to forget, like kissing Sawyer's dirty little bony feet in the ER over and over again. Like talking to him and telling him I was there. At that moment in time, I didn't know the book I would write would be about his death. I hoped it would be about the trial I endured: "that one time Sawyer was in the hospital and *almost* died."

But that's not the book I get to write.

Let's go back to October of 2009. (By the way, from here on out I am officially skipping every October). In October of 2009, I suffered a ruptured ectopic pregnancy. It was critical.

I was at church and suddenly felt like I was going to vomit. I stood up and excused myself to go to the bathroom but passed out. As I fell, my head hit the door. An ambulance rushed me to the hospital and once they figured out what happened, they made the decision to do emergency surgery to remove my ovaries.

My husband Jack was the ecclesiastical leader of our church congregation at the time. He often recounts an experience he had in the hospital. He had said multiple prayers, and the pointed answer he received after completing a prayer in the lonely hospital waiting room was this: "Everything will be all right." His troubled mind wasn't sure whether that meant, "It will be fine because Jaime will live, her organs will not fail as they are threatening to do, but she will be fine and recover." Or if maybe it meant, "It will be fine because you and Jaime are married and can live together forever. She will be leaving this earth, you will be sad, but fine here without her and reunited in time." He said he felt peace but wasn't sure how his life would play out over the next minutes, hours, months, and years. He told me that story in the hospital when I awoke and was officially going to "pull through." It has always made me both sad and happy, knowing when I die, Jack will be able to find a sense of peace.

Sitting in the hospital room with Sawyer in October of 2016, Jack and I both felt a similar response weighing on our hearts. Everything would be all right, but probably not because Sawyer would recover. Rather, it would be "all right," *(used very loosely)*, whatever that ended up meaning, because of the ultimate, if not immediate, belief we hold that families can be together after this life.

Someone told me months after Sawyer passed away that she had a dream Jack and I were standing at a podium in front of a large audience talking about grief, trials, and how to handle it all. I had a moment when she said it, as though a lightning bolt hit straight at my heart. I didn't know how, but I felt there was truth in her dream. I thought, *Maybe I am supposed to write a book about this for the world to share our story.* I have always been blessed with many friends who hold no religious faith and who share a different faith other than my own. I thought, *Maybe I am supposed to share our story to help build a bridge amongst faiths.* I stewed over the notion, but it never felt exactly right.

I have never really fit in a box with regards to who I am as a person. Throughout my life I have worked hard to balance my deep Christian faith with my feminist beliefs. Even as a young child, I was always drawn to doctrines of equality and compassion. In college, as I navigated my faith and my secular beliefs, I was able to hone in on finding a way to articulate my love of God and my understanding of women's rights to help me find what drives me to be my best self. I have often felt this balancing act required me to study and understand both my faith and my feminism in very clear ways to reconcile and meld these two components of who I am and the lens with which I see the world. This melding of my two identities has often blessed me by bringing people at opposite ends of various spectrums together. *Maybe I am supposed to write this book to help build a bridge between the extremely conservative and extremely liberal, helping build a bridge for those of differing perspectives across the board to center on a conversation about various components of healing, grief, and resilience.* I stewed over the notion, and it also didn't feel right. Almost every angle I could think of to tell the story about our family's experience seemed at odds. If I wrote it for the secular world, all the pieces of my story centering on religiosity would need to be watered down and would lose value. If I wrote it for the population of religious book readers, my personality (which at times can be a little testy and perhaps not as Christ-centered as I would like it to be) would need to be watered down and it would lose value.

Then it hit me. I am writing it for me. For my family. For those I love who love Sawyer as well. For the people my children will love who will never get the chance to meet Sawyer in this life. I am writing it for people who never knew Sawyer but who know grief. I am writing it because so many people have said, "Thank you for sharing your grief journey. It is enlightening and helps me understand grief and pain in a better way." This is for anyone who needs to hear our story to feel license to tell their own story. It's for anyone who has the fortunate experience of never living through real grief, perhaps someone who doesn't understand that grief is powerful and can both destroy and build someone up over and over again. It's for people who know grief all too well and need to know they are not alone in their grieving. It is for anyone who wants insight into grief in order to understand their own life a little better, or understand someone they love who is grieving a little better. There is no singular reason for writing this book, nor one singular audience.

Sawyer is the context for this book and the reason I am writing it, but simply exposing our lives to the world is not my ultimate purpose. I have learned something in this grief path I walk. Too many people lack exposure to the dirty underbelly of grief and don't understand what it is like to grieve. I think it is in part because we don't spend enough time with grief and people who are grieving. People avoid the subject and consequently they avoid people who are grieving. They might say the wrong things, hurting grieving people further. Or, in avoidance, say nothing at all, causing the griever to feel ignored. And I get it, believe me. My painful stories fill these pages. Not just mine but lots of people I have met on this journey.

Friends of ours who lost their son after only a few days of living joined a support group for grieving families. As part of their participation, they were given passes for their family to attend Kings Dominion, an amusement park in Virginia. The father was telling a coworker about the passes and the coworker said, "That is awesome. I wish someone would give me free passes to an amusement park!," as though losing a child equates to bonus free fun for all. Obviously, if this coworker recognized how he came across, he would have said something different, or perhaps nothing at all. We don't speak to the grieving enough to know how to speak and what to say and, conversely, what not to say.

I have been in enough book groups in my life to have learned this lesson. There is always the one person that none of us wants to let choose the book. It's the person who always chooses the WWII book, the long and heavy book, the book we save for January because we don't want to read it in the summer when we want something light, nor over the holidays when we want something joyful. We want to read fun books to escape. Or helpful books on subjects we can relate to or that provide insight or information. We don't want to read a book knowing at the onset it is going to be sad. Sadness is bad. Sadness is tough.

But here's the thing. We need to blow the conversation about grief wide open. We need to stop being so worried about the vulnerabilities grief opens up in all of us. We need to embrace Washington Irving's notion about tears. He says, "There is a sacredness in tears. They are not the mark of weakness, but of power. They speak more eloquently than ten thousand tongues. They are the messengers of overwhelming grief, of deep contrition, and of unspeakable love." We need to be able to truly "mourn with those who mourn" and offer comfort to those in need of comforting (Mosiah 18:9, *Book of Mormon*), and that requires understanding, compassion, and empathy. If we never share our experiences with grief and tragedy, we can never have honest discussions about it. Mourning with those in true pain requires more than just dropping off a casserole or posting a kind message on social media. It involves stepping into their shoes. Getting dirty. Seeing the ugly parts and understanding what makes them ugly, and still showing up for each other no matter the cost.

So many people have commented that reading our family's social media comments about grief put them in a better place to lend a hand to other grievers and how grateful they were we were sharing. At first, I thought people were placating us, and maybe some of them were. But I think there's more to it. Yes, sharing served as an outlet to us as grievers so the emotions didn't make us explode. But reading about our life and what we were experiencing helped people build empathy by reading about the ugliness of grief. It seemed to serve the readers by helping them develop empathy in a real-life, get-your-hands-dirty, it's-not-all-rainbows-and-unicorns sort of way.

Part of my religious belief acknowledges there are ways to approach healing, seek peace, and find hope despite the despair we feel surrounding grief. But there is a difference between healing and curing—*there is no cure for grief.* My hope is that this book will help open the conversation about grief. I offer you a glimpse into our tragedy which brought, and brings with it, a lot of messy grief, so that in turn others might know how to better mourn with those who mourn and offer true peace and comfort to those in need.

Before we get into it, there are a few things I need everyone to know about me and my thoughts on grief. This is not an etiquette book on handling grief for mourners. Grief is different for everyone, and I will say that in about a million different ways explicitly and implicitly throughout my story. But it is a real look at how and why it can be difficult to heal from grief. I hope it is a story that will help remove some of the shame people feel about grieving, particularly grieving that others think has "gone on too long." Hopefully reading about our family will give you a sense of how deep some wounds can be, will show you that healing does not mean "moving on" or "getting over it," and that a huge part of living our life in the fullest, best way, means bringing grief along with us on our journey.

# Chapter 1

## *The End*

THE WRITER KAREN BLIXEN (ISAK DINESON) SAID, "ALL SORROWS can be borne if you put them into story or tell a story about them." Is it too early in our relationship for you to hear me call this renowned author a liar? Liar is a strong word, I know, up there with "hate" and "ugly," but as I sob writing almost every word of this book, I wonder if this sentiment is true. I guess I am going to put it to the test and start at the beginning—of the end.

It's funny. Logically it seems like this would be the most difficult part of the story to write so I would put it off until the end. As a family, though, we have always preferred "bad news before good news." I think that's in part why this is the first part of the story. I wanted to get it out of my brain, out of my body. I needed to get it out. It's almost like I am afraid it will disappear or I will forget it. Some days all I want to do is forget it, but then I panic. What have I already forgotten about it? Will I remember it? Will I remember Sawyer and our final moments together? Do I even want to remember? Ultimately, I do.

The end:

> *"Sawyer Holden Clemmer McKinley, 10, a 6th grader at Amelia County Middle School, passed away peacefully on Friday, October 28, 2016. While at school on Wednesday, Sawyer experienced a catastrophic brain hemorrhage from a malformation of the*

*vessels in his brain called Arteriovenous Malformation (AVM). It is a congenital, silent condition until it presents itself, at which time the presentation is usually grave. Sawyer's condition was unknown until it presented itself and he was taken to the hospital where after three brain surgeries, he passed away."*

. . . . . . . . . . . . . . . . .

Sawyer and Jack arrived home in Amelia, Virginia, from their trip to San Diego, California, just before 2 a.m. It was a last-minute decision for Sawyer to go. The previous year Jack's sister Jenny had been diagnosed with an uncommon heart condition and was given a projection of possibly only five years to live. Jack is very close to his eight siblings and decided then he would make greater effort and spend the money and time necessary to visit Jenny as often as he could. As he was booking his ticket one night in early August 2016, on a whim I said, "Why don't you take Sawyer with you?" It just came out of my mouth. Grayson, age 13, and Finn, age 18, Sawyer's older brothers, had both done cross-country trips with their dad and it felt like the time was right for Sawyer to get some long-distance travel time alone with Dad. We booked the ticket and didn't think twice.

They snuck into the house early on the morning of October 26, 2016 without me waking up, which was odd because I am such a light sleeper. When I arose to my alarm to get everyone else ready for school, I let Sawyer sleep. "It's middle school, he has been gone for a week, I'll let the boy get some rest," I rationalized.

I dropped Grayson off at the high school (Sawyer and Grayson both attended middle school together but Grayson had French II first period at the high school). When I got home from the high school drop off, Jack had to leave for work so I got Sterling, our youngest who was three at the time, dressed and took her to preschool. *I will let Sawyer sleep a few extra minutes and will come back and wake him up for school. He will miss Art and Gym and be at school in time for Social Studies. Perfect,* I thought. I left Sawyer home alone at the house while I took Sterling to preschool.

Overwhelming panic arises in me when I think about the fact that not two hours before Sawyer landed in the hospital bed on a gurney he was home alone. *Alone!* What if the AVM had hemorrhaged and ruptured at home while no one was there? What if he had been alone? What if I had found him seizing, or worse, when I arrived home from dropping Sterling off at preschool? What if the only measure of joy (can we call it that?) we have gotten from this loss, our ability to donate his organs, was compromised because the event happened at home and he was at the house too long before getting to surgery to be able to save his organs?

There are so many "what if" moments that could have played out so much more traumatically. I am forever grateful that if it *had* to happen, it happened the way it did. It was a tender mercy. In his talk "Tender Mercies of the Lord," David Bednar says,

> *The Lord's tender mercies are the very personal and individualized blessings, strength, protection, assurances, guidance, loving-kindnesses, consolation, support, and spiritual gifts which we receive from and because of and through the Lord Jesus Christ.*

Jack doesn't like the phrase "tender mercies." He thinks it is cliché or overused or somehow lacks expressing the intimacy of God's personal love because it is such a generic term. But I don't know what else to call the experience of finding small joys in an overwhelming loss, so "tender mercies" wins. Sawyer's AVM rupturing at school and not in my home, as difficult as it made it for so many people, was a tender mercy for which I am grateful.

With everyone out of the house the morning it happened, I was able to awaken Sawyer and give my boy a kiss and hug before I told him to hop in the shower. He showered and came down, but his hair was dry. I gave him a hug and asked him if he had washed his hair. He is a ten-year-old boy, so he said "Um, yeah, sort of." "Well, how come your hair is dry?" *Mumble, mumble, mumble.* I laughed, "Sawyer, I love you and I need you to go back and wash your hair please." "Fine." I sometimes replay this conversation over again in my mind. I'm glad I said, "I love you," and I don't know why I did. I am glad I didn't yell at him or get mad at him. But why did I make him go back and wash his hair? Why couldn't I have just spent those last couple of minutes listening to him tell me about his trip to Legoland while he was with his dad in California, instead of telling him he could recount the events of his trip after school? There is a guilt that plagues me and probably will eternally. Nonetheless, he needed to know I was his mom and I was going to be there for him and I was also going to make him wash his hair. I didn't know what would transpire. We never know what is going to transpire. So do we never make our children wash their hair? I don't think we do. I think we make them take care of their bodies. We make them take pride in their appearance. While we don't throw down the gauntlet every time they appear in an outfit comprised of plaid shorts and striped pants (which Sawyer did, often), we do have a responsibility to love and care for them, even if it is at the expense of other things sometimes. But oh, what I wouldn't give to have those minutes back.

After he was out of the shower for the second time, I went upstairs to check on him. I wanted to make sure he wasn't mad at me for our little hair scuffle and he wasn't. He was brimming with excitement. He could not be contained. He was just bubbling over with story after story about their trip. I was standing in his doorway and he was unpacking his book bag. He had purchased a Pikachu ceramic bank and it was wrapped in layers and layers of clothing. He said, "*Mom!* I have to show you this! I didn't realize I had wrapped it so tightly! Look at this awesome bank I bought in Mexico!" As he unwrapped layer after layer and I stood there in the doorway, I swear to you I heard a voice say in my mind, "Take a snapshot of this moment. These are the moments that define childhood. Take a picture of this moment in your mind so you can be present here in this moment and remember it forever." I swear to you, hand to Bible, I did just that and I thought, *Wow, turning 40 has changed you as a parent, Jaime. Kudos for living in this moment and not caring what the clock says.*

He showed me the piggy bank and a few Pokémon cards he had purchased for his brothers. He also showed me a Charizard toy he bought in Mexico and told me how excited he was to see Grayson and show him all the purchases he'd made. He was glowing. He showed me the T-shirt he had purchased at the beach in San Diego. It was a ridiculous T-shirt! It was gray and had a pug in a hoodie on it and said, "Pug Life." He loved it and was anxious to show his friends and tell them about his trip. I told him, "Come down and grab a bite to eat and I want to take a picture of your absurd shirt." He was all abuzz as he packed his book bag. He didn't want to eat breakfast, he rarely did, so I made him throw back a fig bar anyway. While he sat on the yellow bench tying his aquamarine sneakers, in his red cutoff shorts made from his skinny jeans, I chuckled to myself about his outfit. It was totally hilarious in a totally Sawyer way. It was perfectly him. Never an outfit I would choose for him, but perfectly him. He started to tell me about the details of Legoland and I told him his siblings would want to hear too, so wait and tell us after school. (As an aside, never wait. When someone you love wants to share their joy, let them. He could have told me and he could have told them again later. I will never know what he had to say about so many things, but if I had taken a moment I could have at least heard more of his joy. Never wait.)

I told Sawyer to gather his things and head to the car so we could make it to Social Studies on time. I wrote him a note for being late to class and we got in the car. We were pulling out of our long driveway and I said, "Darn it! I forgot to take a picture of your crazy shirt." He said, "You can get one when I get home from school". I agreed and we proceeded. Then I had a strong impression and said, "No, I'm sorry but just unbuckle and hop out of the car. I really want a picture of you in the shirt now." I put the car in park, he hopped out, and I snapped the shot. One shot. One photo. The lighting was terrible and the background nothing special. *I'll get a better one later.* I took the photo because I wanted it for a Facebook post and thought, *how silly to stop the car and get us both out for a social media moment.* I listened to the promptings of the Spirit the first time and will be forever grateful for that tender mercy. While we were in the hospital, I kept looking at that photo and asking everyone who walked in, "What if this was the last picture I will ever take of my son?" No one had an answer. They all looked at me with the look that I would come to know often as the "we are so sorry but you are now a parent who has lost a child and we are so sad but we don't know what to say so we will nod approvingly and try to not make the moment worse and we will say nothing" look. I still get it a lot.

October 26, 2016, 9:24 a.m. The last photo I ever took of *my* Sawyer.

. . . . . . . . . . . . . . . . . .

We pulled up to the front door of the school. I was in my gym clothes. Now to clarify, I am not the gym clothes wearing type. Some women sport the yoga-pants-athletic-shirt-look in confidence as their muscles glisten in the sunlight for all to see. Not this woman. I am more the "What's the biggest thing I own that I can raise my hands in the air and *not* show my baby-belly that isn't really a baby belly this many years later, but more of a 'donut belly'" gym clothes wearing woman. I didn't want to go into the middle school, but I also wanted it to be a learning moment for Sawyer.

He had just skipped the fifth grade and went straight from elementary school to middle school, so this was his first time being late to middle school. I told him that in elementary school I had to walk him in, but in middle school, children just took the note in and the secretary would give them a pass to go to class. He wasn't sure about it. He asked me to walk him in and I assured him they would let him proceed to class with the note. I even paused and thought about whether or not I should walk him in. I had the distinct thought, *He is learning the power of 'the note from a parent' right now. He is learning independence. But keep tabs on this newfound knowledge of his, he will be the one of all my children to employ this power in a possibly unauthorized way.* I told him that to make him feel comfortable, I would pull forward past the office and wait for him to walk through the office, get his note, and pass down the hall. The hall was mostly made of glass and I promised him I would roll my window down and give him the thumbs-up after I waited for his thumbs-up to indicate the transaction had gone smoothly. He agreed and the interaction went as planned. I can still see him through that smoky glass giving me the thumbs-up when I pull into the middle school parking lot every day now and I hate it. I think, *Why didn't I just walk him in?* **Why didn't I just walk him in?** It brings in to play another round of guilt. This guilt, of course, triggers the rabbit hole.

You know the rabbit hole. You go there yourself sometimes. I start the guilt soundtrack in my head: Why did you let him play video games instead of playing more educational games with him? Why did you ever let him spend time alone? Why did you promote independence from such an early age, he was only ten. Why did you let him play with children who were older, maybe it made him mature too quickly. Why didn't you spend more time reading aloud to him? Why did you ever let that child out of your sight for anything or for anyone? Why? The talking in my head gets louder and louder and the guilt gets heavier and heavier.

My new friend Amy—that's code for my therapist, because not everyone can understand the value of a therapist—said something in our second meeting that I am trying to embrace because I think there is truth to it. Amy asked if Sawyer had never been out of my sight, if he had not been allowed to grow in his independence and in his character, would he still be the same Sawyer that we knew and loved? If I never let him play video games with Lucas down the street, would they have been able to form such a beautiful childlike friendship? Would he be my Sawyer if I had smothered him and never let him explore, let him try things on his own, or even let him be on his own? Probably not. The Sawyer we love is the Sawyer he is because of the way we raised him and because of the boundaries we set and the wings we gave him and there can be no room for regrets. There are too many other burdens to carry now. So, I try to take a measure of comfort in his final thumbs-up. To take comfort in the things I did instead of in the things I didn't do. Finding comfort is not an easy task. But since there are so many things in my new life now that I cannot control, I am trying harder to do better at the things I can control. I am trying to start by letting some of the guilt balloons go. (Cue the *Frozen* soundtrack, right parents? That phrase eternally belongs to Elsa. Thanks, Disney.)

I gave Sawyer the return thumbs-up after seeing his thumb go up through the long, tinted window and I drove away. Nothing is close to our home except more of nothing. That morning, the boys were at school and Sterling was in preschool and I had a long morning free, so I decided to go to the gym to work on that extra weight that I could no longer call a "baby belly." I had actually made my very first appointment with a personal trainer for that morning. I told my husband that "come hell or high water" I was going to find a way in the budget to meet with that trainer and get into shape. I sort of chuckle now because we got the hell and the high water, so I have since banished that saying from my vocabulary entirely.

But that morning, since I was already out dropping off Sawyer at school and had left early to get to my appointment, I figured I could drive a couple miles further out of the way to get the cheap gas for the van. The drive is about twenty minutes so I obviously hadn't checked my phone because I was driving. And then I hadn't checked it because I was pumping gas. But before heading to the gym from the gas station, I pulled my phone out and saw them. The texts. The messages. The missed calls. It was starting.

# Chapter 2

## *The Beginning*

*"Give sorrow words; the grief that does not speak whispers the o'er fraught heart and bids it break."*

—Shakespeare, Macbeth

BEFORE I TELL YOU MORE ABOUT THE STORY OF SAWYER'S DEATH, I feel like I need to tell you a sweet and condensed version of his life.

When Sawyer was born, we had a party! Literally. My doctor came in to check on me in the hospital room after my C-section. The room was full of people, including Sawyer's brothers, Grayson and Finn, who were three and eight at the time. Minutes after Dr. Colby came in to ask me how I was feeling, my sister walked in with a couple of pizzas. Dr. Colby said, "You just had a baby and it is a circus in here, you need your rest." It was a circus, and I wouldn't have had it any other way. My first two deliveries were difficult, touch-and-go vaginal deliveries turned into C-sections. Not wanting to endure those experiences again, I scheduled a cesarean section when I was pregnant with Sawyer. Having scheduled Sawyer's arrival, receiving medicine from the beginning, and feeling better after his birth than I had in nine months, I said, "Bring on the party!" My doctor suggested to me that everyone should leave so I could get the much needed rest my body required. I loved my doctor, thanked him for being so amazing, and told him we'd consider the whole "rest thing." He shook his head and left us to celebrate in our loud and obnoxious way.

Sawyer's life was one big party. Really, it was, ask anyone who knew him. He lit up every room. People gravitated to him. He wasn't a crier; he didn't get upset often. He was filled with smiles and joy and happiness and laughter. His happiness and joy reached a magical level almost all the time. He was the first to surrender his way when he and his siblings disagreed on something. They are going to read this and offer rebuttals, but I am talking about most of the time, not always. He took pleasure in the smiles, the peace, and the joy of life. He radiated laughter and magic. Of course, in his absence I feel this loss of his magic magnified, but as I was preparing photos for a slideshow of his short, full life, I noticed something. I joked we should call the slide show, "Sawyer's Tongue: A Collective." He was always making a crazy face, striking a pose, dancing in a costume, or all of the above. It wasn't just for the camera either, it was just how he lived his life.

Sawyer was a daredevil from the very beginning. When he was around eighteen months old, he was climbing over the playground equipment like it was programmed into his DNA, like dexterity or development had nothing to do with it. My neighbor Paige would go crazy watching him when we went to the park together. Constant gasping, holding her breath, closing her eyes, and gesturing a catching movement while at the edge of her seat did not make playtime relaxing for her. Sawyer made her nervous. He made everyone nervous because he was always testing the limits of his abilities. But I had spent almost every waking moment with him for those eighteen months and I knew one thing: Sawyer knew his limits, almost innately. Most of the time. He was all adventure and experimentation, no hesitation, and definitely no fear.

He was the magic in every room and the life of every party. He understood wit and sarcasm from an early age. I remember his third-grade teacher telling us once, "Sawyer is smart. Too smart. He gets everything and I forget. Once I was telling another teacher a story and when I hit the punch line, the other teacher started to chuckle and I heard another tiny voice from the other side of the classroom also start to quietly laugh. Sawyer had heard my story and thought it was funny. The other kids in the room had no idea what I was talking about.

Sawyer picks up on everything." Such was often the case, Sawyer understanding much more than people were aware, including myself and his father. He taught me the meaning of the word "cudgel." He taught his dad the meaning of the word "peckish." His backpack was always loaded down with the biggest books, a skill he learned from his older brothers. His brothers wouldn't let him watch a movie based on a book until he had read the book, so they kept him reading. Finn would start a series, Grayson would follow. Then we would tell Sawyer, "You are a little young. In a couple of years you can read the series too." We would turn around and sure enough, Sawyer would be into book three of whatever series the brothers had just completed. There was no stopping his quest for brilliance.

· · · · · · · · · · · · · · · · ·

"Classic Sawyer." A phrase any one of us would employ when Sawyer did something absolutely outrageous, from something mildly funny all the way to hilarious, or beyond what the rest of us would deem as rational or appropriate. This was not a rare occurrence. After Sawyer died, one of his friends from the soccer team told us a "Classic Sawyer" story. One morning at school, during the morning announcements over the PA system, the librarian said, "Someone has mistakenly taken the most popular princess book from the library and needs to return it immediately." Sawyer, without skipping a beat, stood up and walked to his backpack and headed out as though he were the one who had taken the book. Everyone laughed. Sawyer could make even the grumpiest of us smile.

A favorite "Classic Sawyer" series of unfortunate comical events took place at the end of the school year. For three years. On the last day of school, the last three years of his life, he was in urgent care for an outrageous stunt. We used to joke that Sawyer needed a "frequent flier" card for BetterMed. Go figure, the joke lost its flair after October 2016.

The first year, Sawyer was in the second grade and school was dismissed early. Attention all administrators: nothing good ever happens on early release days. We were in the process of moving to Amelia, Virginia, from Radford, Virginia, and so boxes were everywhere.

Sawyer thought it would be a good experiment to see what would happen if he got in a twenty-gallon plastic bin and tried surfing down the stairs.

Hypothesis: It will be awesome! Result: Urgent Care.

The doctor said, "I will be shocked if he doesn't have a break, or multiple breaks, in his arm and shoulder." Consider the doctor shocked and baffled. No breaks, no fractures, just a lot of terrible bruises and a humongous smile on Sawyer's face. He said, "Take a picture of my black and blue shoulder and back and send it to Dad and Grandpa Bob!"

The second year, Sawyer was in the third grade and the children were having their end of the year BBQ in the county field across the street from the school. I got a call from Jack: "Come to the county lot, Sawyer has been hit in the face with a football and he is going to need stitches." I dashed over there as they were putting Sawyer in Jack's car to rush him to urgent care. He was crying, which was so unusual for Sawyer. He had such a high pain tolerance and didn't show sadness often, so I knew he was seriously hurt. Jack said Sawyer calmed down in the urgent care office and only cried when they gave him a shot to numb his face. Eight stitches in the face. He had a resulting scar and fat lip he thought was so cool. The doctors said it would eventually heal and flatten out, but it would take several years. Several years he did not get.

For those counting, there is still the final event in his series of Last Day Shenanigans. The third year, Sawyer was in the fourth grade and the children were playing out on the playground one last time. As fourth graders, they would be promoted to the middle school building as their own fifth grade entity of the elementary school. No playground. I have no doubt Sawyer was using his last moments of recess to their fullest. Another call came to my phone from the school nurse. (Side note: I have stopped answering calls from the district nurse. Just kidding, Social Services, I answer every time!) "I think Sawyer has broken his arm." "How?" I asked. "He says he was playing on top of the monkey bars and the kids yelled there was a giant bug on his shoulder so he swatted it and fell off." It sounded fishy, but not entirely out of the realm of possibility for Sawyer, and it didn't matter because the broken arm was the issue, not the reason. So back we went to urgent care, where, by this point, they loved Sawyer. The x-rays revealed a possible break and the orthopedic doctor confirmed it. We were slated to leave for the Dominican Republic just a couple short weeks later so they agreed to cut the cast off at four weeks so he could travel unencumbered. We opted for the waterproof cast. (Parents: always opt for the waterproof cast, it will be the best out of pocket $50 you spend.) One of my favorite pictures is of Sawyer on the diving board at the swimming pool doing flips into the pool, in his cast.

Addendum to the 4th grade story: At his Celebration of Life, we allowed anyone, including his friends, to come up and tell a story or share a Sawyer moment with the audience. Many were too sad, too shy, or too shocked to come up to the stage but there were a few children who braved the pulpit. One friend even came up twice. We learned at that time that his fall from the monkey bars might not have actually been caused by "swatting a bug." While there may have been a bug, there had also been a girl. A girl who, while they were playing tag, pushed him off the monkey bars. Truth revealed! The earlier story never quite made sense. To hear this revelation at his Celebration of Life made us all laugh through our tears, and it was just the levity we needed to get through the rest of the service. Sawyer had been protecting his friend from the trouble she might be in for contributing to his broken arm. It was a perfect revelation at the perfect moment. I will always be grateful for the brave children, and adults, who set their fears and sadness aside to give our family one more moment with our sweet boy.

I want everyone who reads this book to know everything about Sawyer. I know this is impossible. I want them to know his favorite food was tacos, with lots of hot sauce. I want them to know he was into sports and video games and Pokémon. I want them to know he was a prankster to the utmost. I want them to know every funny story and every beautiful thing about him. But ask any parent who has lost a child and they also want the world to know about their child. Some parents who have lost children don't have any stories to tell, because they were taken from this earth only a few hours old. Some parents who have lost children have only sad stories to tell because their child's life was filled with harsh realities, doctor visits, hospital stays, and pain. I have learned this about children who have died and the parents who love them. While we have many things that make us different, we all share one thing: we all want more time and more stories.

So, if you have stories of someone who has died, share them with their loved ones. Write them down and give them a copy. Make copies of pictures you have. I love hearing old stories. Tell them, often. Sometimes people say, "Oh, I didn't want to mention Sawyer or tell the story because I didn't want to make you sad." I am sad. Tell the story. Always tell the story and always say their name. I tell everyone who is willing to say his name or share a memory it will bring a tear to my eye and a song to my heart. Plus, any story or memory you have might be new. The stories I have about Sawyer are finite now. But the notion that there is a story or photo out there of Sawyer that I have never heard, something that could be new to me, it's a dream. Make someone's dream come true and share the story.

. . . . . . . . . . . . . . . . . .

When I reflect on Sawyer's short life, which is almost constantly, I think about all of the terrible ways the AVM that took his life could have manifested its unwelcome presence earlier. What if the AVM had stolen Sawyer from us in a demonstration of "Classic Sawyer?" As a mother, I have had a difficult time trying to forgive myself for not cracking down on his outrageous behavior, for not metaphorically leaning in to catch him somehow, for not limiting the limitless boundaries he set for himself. As if that somehow would have mattered or impacted how he died or when he died, but truth tells me otherwise. That AVM determined Sawyer's path long before I parented him. But one of the crazy components of grief is that it makes you think and feel irrational thoughts. It's one of the powers grief holds over people. The "what if's" are brutal.

Somehow our family was gifted with this amazing child who loved, of all things, sports. His favorite sport was soccer. To the world this may not seem like a rarity, a child who loves sports. However, if you knew the rest of our family, you'd know we are a bit anti-sports. My father-in-law called us "sports snobs" and we kind of were, but not in the way you'd think. It wasn't in the "some sports or athletes are better than others." Rather it was that sports and athletes were somehow inferior. It probably stemmed from us being last picked in PE, unathletic, and generally uninterested in sports altogether. Our disinterest over time took the shape of superiority, which Sawyer made us confront. Sawyer loved everything sports, and we loved him, and somehow the transference began. Don't get me wrong, we had always enrolled our children in the requisite recreational league soccer teams and the occasional basketball leagues for the exercise, but we were never sports oriented. We always scratched our heads as we watched Sawyer excel at every sport he tried, wondering where his natural ability came from, recognizing the sports gene must be recessive.

Everything Sawyer learned about sports, he learned from his friends, mostly from his bosom buddy and doppelganger, Brody. I remember when Sawyer came home from school for days in a row talking about Clay Matthews. I thought he was someone from school and finally had to research him. Even for this paragraph I had to Google "famous Green Bay Packers player" because I couldn't recall his name, but I knew I would recognize it. (*And I did!*)

Sawyer's birthday is February 3, and it always either fell on or near Super Bowl Sunday. Not being a sports-watching family, we decided when he was about five that our gift to him would be to all watch the Super Bowl together, for the entire game. The rules were: 1) no leaving early, 2) you had to pick a team to cheer for, and 3) no reading a book, even during commercials. We would watch, and cheer, and eat a feast of junk food chosen by the birthday boy. I don't know how we are ever supposed to watch the Super Bowl again, but in time I imagine we will, because we love our sports-loving son. Sawyer taught me to be open to new things, and even when we don't find our passion in them, we can find joy being with others who do.

Sawyer always wanted to play football himself and not just watch. We never let him. We used to joke, "At least we know what Sawyer will resent us for when he is an adult: the fact that we never let him throw on a helmet and join a football team." We cited all of these studies about brain trauma, the football culture of sexism, and the fact that Sunday football didn't really mesh with our religious observance of Sundays in general. Go figure, the child didn't really accept any of those reasons. I am sure he talked about us as terrible parents to anyone who would listen, but I do feel like he respected us for our decision because he never gave us too much flak for it. He was persistent in his request each year but accepted our refusal.

Our substitution was that we supported him in his love of soccer. I think some of his love for soccer came as transference from football, but he loved playing soccer. I read an article once that talked about how to encourage your children in sports. (Because as a non-athlete, of course the best way to understand a sport is to read a newspaper article about it.) The article counseled parents to say, "I love watching you play" instead of "You did a great job." I would say that often to him, and it was genuine. I loved watching my boy play soccer. And basketball. And I would find myself yelling loudly and proudly (and angrily at times when the ref was inept, which was confusing to me because I thought I didn't care . . .) at his games. I was transforming. I didn't love sports, but I did love watching Sawyer play. He would glide down the field and I would smile from ear to ear. He thrived in his element, albeit an element foreign to me. I will never forget the basketball game where he scored 30 baskets (!) in one game. He was on fire! I am sad so many people in the world will never see him move across another court or field, driven and determined.

Sawyer was known in soccer, even from his first season, for his crazy headers. This was before everyone was all crazy (read, *smart!*) about concussions in children and they banned headers under a certain age. From halfway up the field, he would run and hit that ball with his head and it would fly away. When I think about how Sawyer died, and about how he had three brain surgeries to try and save him, and how in the end, the big, beautiful brain that made him the magical person he was is the very thing that killed him, I don't know how to feel.

. . . . . . . . . . . . . . . . .

Sawyer was adventurous and brave. Those were his defining traits. He would not have been the same Sawyer we knew and loved if we had not let him develop into his daredevil self. I think about how I would've parented Sawyer differently if I had known about his brain AVM. Would I have let him climb the high ladder to keep up with his brothers on the playground? Would I have let him chase the dog faster and further than any three-year-old should've been able to run? Would I have even let him join any team sports, never seeing him thrive and excel? To possibly have seen his death as the result of him doing something he loved or acting in a way that defined who he was as a person would have taken me to an entirely other epic level of mother guilt. I am not sure I would have been able to handle it. Sawyer lived the fullest life possible, including the best final week of life anyone could ever hope for, and that in and of itself is a tender mercy we will always hold dear. If the AVM had to take him, I am grateful it took him in Social Studies class instead of on the soccer field.

To survive this journey, I have to continue to acknowledge the tender mercies along the way. That said, please never tell anyone who is grieving how much worse it could have been, or "at least . . ." There is no "at least" in child loss. How much more traumatic for us, and for how many more children, if Sawyer had been rushed to the hospital during a soccer game? After he'd been pushed off the monkey bars? Or after he'd been pushed by a bully after scoring too many hockey goals? What if it'd happened when we were in a foreign country? Maybe while he was sliding down the rocks into a waterfall headfirst? (All real examples of his outrageousness.) Or what if it had happened playing football? What if it happened any time or in any place where I as a parent had control over what he was doing, and he was doing something deemed too risky? That was most of his life: Sawyer was not a bench sitter.

If you Google "AVM" (*don't*) one thing it says is the malformations usually manifest starting at age ten all the way up to age forty. Ten. This stupid, terrible, silent killer did exactly what it was supposed to do. I guess it is gratitude, but I am so grateful for the ten spectacular years we got with Sawyer and grateful this killer didn't cheat and come any earlier. Of course, my close frenemy, guilt, is never far away. I asked the doctors a million questions.

- Should we have never flown with him? He had been on tons of flights.
- Should we have seen it coming? He was caught up with all his shots and had been to the doctor often for regular childhood illnesses, but we had never seen a clue.

- Should we have not let him play soccer? He had been playing and playing well for years.
- What should we have done differently to have been able to walk out of that hospital with Sawyer in a cast and turn this tragedy into just another story we would laugh about?

Nothing. We could have done nothing. We had absolutely no control and that is not something I handle well.

# Chapter 3

## *The Middle*

THIS STORY OF MINE, AND OF MY FAMILY, AND OF MY BEAUTIFUL BOY is not an easy story to tell. The telling is made harder because I don't know exactly whose story I'm sharing. Is it Sawyer's story, a full-of-life ten-year-old whose time on earth was cut way too short? Is it mine and my husband's story, as parents and a couple who never planned to live out our lives in this way? Is it the story of Sawyer's siblings, Finn, Grayson, and Sterling, all of whom were thrust into this life path of grief, sorrow, and loss much too young? Is it Sawyer's relatives' story, relatives who not only lost Sawyer but also lost the daughters, sons, siblings, and grandchildren they knew so well, because none of us are the same anymore? Yes, it is all of our story. It is also the story of our community. Our new community, knowing us only peripherally for two years, who banded together to make sure we didn't suffer alone. It's the story of our old community, who, despite being geographically far away, didn't forget us and the impact Sawyer had on them as he spent his childhood there. It's a story so much bigger than me and my family. It's the story of people who came together to surround and lift a family in their tragedy. And it is ultimately the story of our collective survival.

Just before he left for his trip to California the week before he passed away, I had taken Sawyer to the library to grab a couple of books for the journey. I wanted him to check out two books, but he insisted on five. I agreed, with the idea that he would take two on the trip and come home and finish the other three. He was reading the HQ series by Ron Smith, but our local library didn't have the one he needed and we didn't have time to order it by mail, so he found a couple others to check out.

Jack called me a couple of days into the trip and said, "Sawyer brought a ton of books in his suitcase. He told me you said he could only bring two, but he snuck four." Sawyer always wanted to know more, but on the sly. His brothers wore their badge of nerdiness like a medal of honor, but Sawyer wanted to be "cool" and nerdiness didn't fit the profile. But he could play a game of chess like nobody's business, name Pokémon cards like he was a gym leader, define words many adult wordsmiths didn't know, and would cite a statistic on almost anything you could suggest, trash talking along the way. He just didn't want his friends to know.

His need to hide his, shall we call it, "scholarly side," was for us part of the shock we experienced in the spring of 2016. Sawyer approached us and asked to skip the fifth grade. "Okay, what Disney show were you just watching?" we asked. "No, I am serious. I have never really felt challenged, I am bored in school, and I just want to see if I can maybe do something I have to work at instead of breeze through." Well, ok then. Jack and I talked about it and decided we would let it go for a little while and see if his urge would blow over. Time passed and as the end of the school year approached, he broached the subject again. We were concerned he would take some flak because Jack was the Superintendent of Schools and Sawyer might get accused of being promoted because of Jack's leadership position in the district.

"What about your friends?" we asked. Sawyer responded, and I quote: "I think my education is more important than friends. I can always make new friends. Besides, if they are mean to me about it, they weren't really my friends." Sawyer was right, he always could make friends, and he did. After a lot of testing, talking, and prayerful consideration, we worked with middle school administration who also felt it would be in Sawyer's best interest to promote him to the sixth grade.

In the aftermath of everything, we recognize his promotion as a tender mercy for all of us. Sawyer, even if only for a short time, was able to experience the illustrious zeitgeist of middle school. He will never see high school and the choices and freedoms those years would have offered him. There are lists upon lists of all the things he will never be able to do. But because of his persistence, tenacity, ability to advocate for himself, in conjunction with a progressive principal interested in the needs of the child over the hassle of designing a new school schedule, Sawyer was able to be a middle school student. He made the first six weeks "All-A honor roll." He joined the golf team, even if he had a broken arm for most of the season. He had a locker (on the bottom, by the way, which he complained about endlessly since he was so tall). He was able to continue a petition his brother began the year earlier to abolish the period of remediation/acceleration most of the students hated. He was able to choose an elective (Art, which he loved). He was able to change classes.

For any parent who has or has had a middle school student, those were all small moments. In hindsight, each of them were tiny miracles for my boy. My unique, one of kind, nobody like him, SoyBoy. When I let panic take hold, sometimes before I can pray for peace and let the calm settle on my soul, I think about what would have been different if we hadn't listened to Sawyer. If we had brushed off his request and denied his appeal to advocate on his behalf with the school. For him in his day-to-day life, probably not much would have been different. He wasn't into the current school year long enough to see a real academic benefit of skipping a grade and he loved his friends in the lower grade so he would have coasted by enjoying the moments of each day. But for Jack and me there would have been a world of difference. We wouldn't have been able to watch him flourish in his maturity as he got involved, even if only for a short while, in all the things the sixth-grade advancement brought. By advocating for him though, listening to him and acting on his worthy desires, we were able to say we did our best as parents in that situation. Mostly, by advocating for him, it gave him a chance to squeeze a little more out of life and cram in a few extra experiences in his short ten years.

Six months after Sawyer died, Jack was asked to give a mini-TED talk type presentation at a statewide superintendent conference. He talked about our experience with Sawyer and how advocating for what is best for the child, not what is easiest for the adult, was time consuming, a bit of a hassle, and involved several players and components, but was, in the end, always worth it. It made such a difference for us as his parents to see Sawyer participate in things he never would have been able to do otherwise because of his young death. Sometimes it is easier to say "no." Most times in fact. Saying "yes" to a loved one, a coworker, a neighbor, whoever, involves action and usually actions that were unplanned or unprepared for which leads to work. None of us are looking for extra work. But I think we are all looking to be better parents, coworkers, neighbors, people, and it comes at a price. The price is a little (let's be real, *sometimes a lot*) of extra work. Sometimes the payoff is that your child gets to advance a grade, be challenged in his workload, meet scads of new friends, and join the golf team. Sometimes there is no immediate payoff (your child dies in spite of every effort by everyone to keep that from happening), but at least you know you tried your hardest and did everything within your power to advocate for the one you love. That knowledge brings a priceless sense of contentment.

Advocating for Sawyer became something we were all too familiar with in the hospital over the five days we were there. Advocating for a loved one often pushes those doing the advocating into uncomfortable positions, questioning boundaries and decisions, and definitely stepping outside of our comfort zone. It did for us, for me anyway. We were constantly asking questions, challenging neurologists, and even begging for someone to do something more. When I was in the hospital in 2009 with my ruptured ectopic pregnancy and was in a coma, Jack spent hours in the waiting room alone. At one point he was exhausted, stinky, and starving, not to mention worried about our children at home, so he called his sister Jenny, who was across the country, and asked for advice. He wanted to go home and regroup and check on things and she said, "You can't. You can't leave that hospital. No matter how much they want her to live, in the end, she is just another patient to them. She is your wife, and they will never care as much as you do if she lives or dies. You have to stay there and make sure every decision, dose, and diagnosis they make is going to get her one step closer to coming home." He stayed. We stayed at the hospital the entire time Sawyer was there to advocate for him and his success, no matter what that success looked like.

The hospital was the worst. But it was also the best. Grief seems to be filled with paradoxes: happy and sad, sorrowful and thankful, best and worst. All of these paradoxes continue to occupy the same space, even though it seems impossible. I remember the first time I learned you could hold joy and sorrow in the same space: I was about four-teen and the movie Steel Magnolias came out. I don't even remember the exact scene but the emotional experience imprinted on me. The character played by Julia Roberts had died as a young mother and the women who were her support network were standing around after the service. The audience, namely me, was in tears at this raw exposure to an untimely death. As I cried, the dialogue changed from sad to happy as the resident curmudgeon said something funny that made the other characters laugh through their tears. But it wasn't just the actresses laughing, the audience was laughing. I was laughing as tears were coming down my face. Little did my naive fourteen-year-old self know that these paradoxical feelings were just an introduction to the subject. Expertise would come twenty-six years later.

In the hospital at the end of his life, I vividly remember caressing the scar on his lip from when the football hit him on the last day of school the year prior. It was a perfect place to touch. His lips were dry and cracked because of all the tubes he was connected to for the surgeries and monitoring and breathing. The nurses were so kind and treated his little face with such love and devotion. They would brush his teeth, put Vaseline on his lips and rib him about his bad breath. He wasn't there. The state of Virginia had declared him dead. I knew his spirit was no longer with us anymore, but the shell of the boy I had birthed and raised was lying next to me and was haggard. Those nurses took care of him for three days as if he was there. They were attentive to everything they did for him. They gave me those last days with him, in that bed, as though he was the most important person in the world. To me, he was. I will forever adore those individuals who brushed his jacked-up little teeth, moistened his scarred-up little lip, and cared for his tiny little body up until the end.

After the first two brain surgeries were unsuccessful at alleviat-ing the pressure in his brain, the neurologist again came in to talk with us about Sawyer. It wasn't looking good. He had been unrespon-sive for too long. His brain was swollen and had nowhere to go. The neurologist explained to us that it was like a watering hose trying to connect to a fire hydrant. The veins had ruptured and the incident, when it started in the school with the seizure, was the beginning of the definite end. The middle was just a natural progression of things. Was there nothing more they could do? "Please, try anything you can!" we pleaded, we begged. They were going to try one final surgery that would involve removing a portion of his skull with the idea that if they could get the swelling down while there wasn't any pressure against his skull, they might be able to save him. I knew at this point that they were doing this as a last-ditch effort and I also knew by their tone and their eyes that they were doing this for us. Yes, of course, they were doing it to say they tried literally everything to bring back my sweet boy. We also knew, with the first two surgeries proving unsuccessful, that even if Sawyer did survive, we would not get our Sawyer back. We knew he would be a broken vestige of our "Classic Sawyer." They indeed did the last surgery and we all waited.

We waited and nothing changed. We waited and nothing happened. We thought our time of advocating was over and we began to vacillate with the decision of how we would ever make the final decision: to end the life of our brain-dead child. We talked to every doctor imaginable. We waited. We talked to more doctors and we waited. We asked questions and more questions and we waited. We cried and prayed and cried and prayed some more. We understood he would never regain consciousness. He would never breathe on his own again. He would never flex his tiny muscles and say with a gleam of sarcasm in his eye, "This is how a real man does it," again. He would never jump out from behind a door and scare me to tears. He would never open his sweet baby blues again. Sawyer was gone and processing this was impossible, so we waited, hoping to make the impossible possible. The moment of full comprehension we were hoping for—accepting Sawyer's death—never came but we still waited. In the middle of the crisis there was nothing more we could do, so we waited. We waited, we know now, so that our hearts could prepare us for the next step of our traumatic journey: the donating.

# Chapter 4

# *The Donating*

WHEN YOU ARE DATING SOMEONE AND EVERYTHING IS FRESH AND new and exciting, you talk about everything. At least Jack and I did while we were dating. We talked constantly. In fact, it was one of the things that clued my mother into the idea that perhaps Jack and I were getting serious. One night I was talking to my mother on the phone during our courtship and she said, "You and Jack must be getting serious." I asked her why she thought that, and she said, "Because you keep mentioning you are hanging out or talking on the phone with him all the time and he doesn't seem to drive you crazy yet." It's true. I was turned off so easily by so many little things when I was dating people in college. Jack and I spent almost all of our spare moments together from the time we met. (The time we met in college anyway, which is my version of when and how we met. Jack and I have different versions of how and when we met, but I will spare you the controversy for now.) Never though, not once, did we discuss what decisions we would make about putting our child on life support following a fatal brain complication. Never did we talk about how long we would allow our child to be hooked up to machines to keep him alive and say goodbyes. Never did we talk about how we would rebound after our entire world came crashing down. We spent a lot of time playing SCRABBLE at the park or hiking around the mountains of St. George, Utah talking about what our lives would look like if we got married. We talked about who would stay home with the kids, who would go back to graduate school first, where we would live, where we would retire. We talked politics and religion as we courted and grew in our relationship. But the decisions we had to make in those few days at the hospital, each one with increasing frequency and impact, were decisions we were ill prepared to make.

It was after three surgeries and after the doctor had come in and spoken with us about final time lines and Sawyer's status, that we started to realize what it all meant for him and for us. Sawyer's young doctor came into our room with a colleague (who was clearly not a doctor) and asked us if this mysterious colleague could talk to us about something. Through the whole event, Sawyer's main doctor had been knowledgeable and informative, forthcoming, compassionate, encouraging without being sugary, realistic without being curt or abrasive, helpful without crossing lines or boundaries. I knew as soon as the words came out of her mouth what she was going to ask. I could just sense it.

She talked to us about the fact that Sawyer was gone and he would never be able to take a breath or have a thought again. She also talked about the corollary fact that his body was strong, healthy, and housing organs that could give life to a bunch of other children and young adults. She asked the question we couldn't fathom: would we consider donating his organs? Honestly, I don't remember exactly how she said it, but that is the gist of what she said. It infuriated me that God had created such a complex system of working parts in humans that, when controlled by the brain, was miraculous in the things it could accomplish. And yet, without the brain, the body could do nothing. I wanted to go down the sci-fi road and envision brain transplants, 3D printed brains, anything. It sounds crazy and callous and I know because I thought those things too. But rational thoughts aside, I remember what I said. "Please! Please Jack, can we do this? Can we please get some measure of *joy/comfort/peace* out of this terrible sorrow?"

I am listed as an organ donor and have been since I was sixteen. Jack was not. He didn't have a problem with me being an organ donor (in fact, he understood the science and logic in his head perfectly) but he couldn't get around the "icky" details of organ donation. So, when Sawyer's doctor presented it, I thought Jack would be my hurdle. But as it turns out, tragedy changes you. I remember what Jack said too. He was hesitant: "I don't know, it just weirds me out." I countered, "Doesn't it weird you out to think about bugs and decomposition taking all of the precious organs we created and Sawyer used?" I remember having and expressing the distinct thought, "What if the child who is going to cure cancer is laying on a hospital bed somewhere with a failing heart? What if some parents can be spared the heartache and the sorrow of living this hell?" We came to realize that organ donation was our miracle. It meant that someone, not us, would get the call we were hoping to get. They would get the visit from the doctor telling them the words we would've traded our own lives for: "Your child is going to live." It wasn't our miracle, but organ donation would give us some miracles. Seven in fact.

We have always been a family who discusses everything, almost to a fault. After I had my ruptured ectopic pregnancy and we knew I would not be able to have more children, we still felt strongly about another child coming to our family. After much pondering, searching for answers, many prayers and many, many sleepless nights, Jack and I decided we should pursue the route of adoption. We wanted input from everyone and called a family meeting to talk to the boys about our desires and impressions to bring a child into our family through adoption. (The details of that story are complicated and miraculous, but for another book, so bear with me.) From that point on in our family, any time we called a family meeting to discuss something important, someone would chime in, "Are we adopting another sibling?"

So, there we were, at the hospital making this monumental decision about Sawyer and we knew Grayson and Finn needed to be involved. Sterling, the daughter we adopted as the result of our biggest family council meetings, was too young for many of these decisions, which was both a blessing and a curse. We called the boys and told them we needed to have a family meeting over the phone, explained what we were considering, and asked what they thought about it. Instantly, truly in the next breath, immediately, Grayson spoke up, very upset because of what it meant for Sawyer. But so resolutely he said, "I was hoping you would do that, I just wasn't sure it was possible." Finn said, "I hadn't even considered it, but I love the idea. Please do it." My children. My innocent, loving, thrust-into-tragedy-like-few-youth-their-age children had given us the confirmation we needed to allow Sawyer to be the hero we knew him to be. With their blessing, our family was able to make the decision to offer seven of our Sawyer's organs to children in need of life.

The decision to donate his organs meant a whole new round of chaos, decisions, paperwork, and time spent at the hospital. After speaking with the boys, Jack and I took a private moment and went out to the courtyard in the PICU. We said a prayer and asked for confirmation of our decision and we felt the most powerful, maybe even the only, moment of peace for us while we were at the hospital. We knew Sawyer would be an organ donor no matter what our emotional cost. The decision had been made and we knew it to be the right decision, but it was still an almost impossible decision. It was terribly hard to consider what organ donation would mean. In part, for me, it meant literal pieces of Sawyer, parts of my very DNA, would be walking around on this earth and not be with me. It meant Sawyer's heart might be pumping in the basketball champion playing the winning game in which Sawyer would never get to compete. His lungs would help someone breathe fresh air in countries and places Sawyer would never be able to go. His kidneys would help some child pee on a bush in their front yard even when their mother told them not too, an act of defiance Sawyer and I would never be able to argue about again. I was having a hard time with it, again, still knowing it was right, but struggling.

It was then, during this struggle, that we got a visit from Jack's coworker and his wife, the Upadhyayas. They had heard the news about Sawyer and had come to lend some emotional support and physical sustenance. Looking back, I chuckle because they brought the best snacks for us at that time. So many people were amazingly thoughtful and made sure we weren't starving, and yet we were starving. Nothing was worth eating. But somehow the snacks they brought were just what we needed to sustain us.

When security called and asked if the Upadhyayas could come up, we of course said yes. While we were waiting for them to arrive in our room, Jack said, "Anu is a very private person and I assume his wife is as well. They may not say much but I know it is a huge deal for them to be here and them coming is such a gesture of support, so just know that and recognize they might not stay long or say anything too personal but their being here is huge." After initial hugs and tears, Shalini insisted on taking me out for fresh air. I kept saying I didn't want to leave Sawyer's bedside, but she promised she wouldn't keep me away long and that I needed fresh air. I conceded and we walked around the PICU courtyard. I took a seat and she sat next to me. I said, "May I ask you very personal questions? You don't have to answer if you are uncomfortable." (You know me, moments after Jack told me they are very private people, I proceeded to totally ignore him.) Anu had helped me a year earlier with a project I was working on for Sawyer's class about different religions, so I knew he and his wife Shalini were Hindu. In that moment at the hospital, I needed to talk to someone who had a little distance from the event, but who I knew to be religious. Shalini was thoughtful and religious, even if hers was a perspective different than my own. In fact, that different perspective was something I didn't know I needed but was desperate to hear.

I forged ahead with my questions. "Are you Hindu and if so, do you believe in cremation?" She paused. It was a long pause. I could tell she was thoughtful and indeed private, but in her kindness she shared her feelings. "We are Hindu and we do believe in cremation." "Even for little children?" I asked as I wept. "Yes, even for children." I asked, "And it's, okay, you think?" She said, "I do," and she hugged me tightly. It was such an intimate moment with a stranger and it brought me such relief. We sat in silence in the dark night for what seemed like a long time, but was probably only a couple of minutes. She then began, "Since you asked me about cremation, we also believe in reincarnation." She proceeded to tell me a very sacred and personal story while sharing with me her theology. I remember she said, "As a mother, you might be somewhere with someone and you just know. You may get an overwhelming sense that Sawyer is with you, Sawyer is with that person you are engaging with and no one else will know. No one else will feel it, but you will feel it and you will know he lives on in that person." In that moment, a powerful witness came to me. Sawyer would absolutely be an organ donor. It reaffirmed our decision, and I saw how Sawyer's body would live on in a sense and it would be okay. I do not believe in reincarnation. But I do believe in an afterlife. I do believe Sawyer's spirit lives on and that he is doing important work on the other side. I am flabbergasted that someone I hardly know was able to share her feelings about life and death and its sacredness at a time when I needed to hear it. Moreover, while we do not share the same faith, the way she shared her testimony of her beliefs helped me solidify my own testimony of the things I believe. There is such power in the intimacy of sharing and listening and understanding. I am forever grateful to Shalini, a very private person, for opening herself up, sharing her beliefs, and helping me understand my own beliefs. I will forever see the exchange of beliefs and ideas in a different way now.

As an aside, sometimes I get overwhelmed with the notion of sharing religious beliefs and how I don't want to "force my ideas down someone else's throat," but I also want to share something I love that I feel like improves my life. What a naïve perspective. I realized God needs to communicate with me any way He can. Sometimes it is through reading our scriptures, through impressions put into our mind, sometimes it is through our family or friends, and sometimes it is through your husband's coworker's wife, a Hindu biology professor, someone you barely know. If we close ourselves off to people who are different, whose ideas seem "other" than our own, we could very easily be shutting down a line of communication with God Himself.

Shalini and I composed ourselves and went back into Sawyer's room. We hugged, said goodbye, and Jack and I called in the organ donor representative. Typically, with organ donation cases (or so we were told—it was our first rodeo) you are assigned a case worker who works a twenty-four-hour shift so he or she can accompany you through the entire process. Our case worker was Kate. She was Italian, she was young, she was bright and bubbly, and she was a ray of sunshine. Well, sardonic sunshine. The only way we could handle everything thrown at us was to go into full clinical sarcastic mode. Jack and I are quite adept at that mode. She could handle us; she could take our biting and somewhat inappropriate humor. She brought a relatable face to the organ donation process and was able to interact with us in a way that put us at ease.

The process involved questions. So many questions! We laughed because we thought when we were going through the adoption process for Sterling there were a lot of questions, and there were, but they were *nothing* in comparison to the questions involved in organ donation. We had to answer questions about our medical history, about Sawyer's medical history, about his life and our life and his health and our health and the list goes on and on. Part of the questioning had to do with Sawyer's last week of life and what he had done, what he had eaten, where he had been. Those questions were obviously distressing. And once the horrible paperwork was completed, another clock started ticking.

In the state of Virginia, for Sawyer to be an organ donor, he had to have an extensive series of tests run followed by repetition of the same tests twelve hours later. Only then could he be declared legally deceased and the organ donation tests could begin. The twelve hours of waiting were excruciating. It was the strangest twelve hours. We knew Sawyer was gone and his spirit was no longer in his body, and we were devastated. Destroyed. There are no words in the English language to describe how we felt. We were all of those adjectives that don't even exist that could express how awful we were. At the same time, we were hopeful, and we put all of our hope in the next basket, which was his ability to donate. We needed him to stay strong. We needed his body to remain strong. Nurses and technicians came in often, several times every hour, to test everything to make sure his organs were staying healthy and not deteriorating. I cannot describe the agony of knowing your son is dead but cheering on his frail little body to be strong enough to give someone else the chance of living. It is a feeling complicated beyond this world. Kate would come in and out with her cheerful yet somber disposition to update us on the progress of finding recipients for his organs. She said she doesn't get many cases like this, with someone so strong and healthy that so many of his organs could be gifted to others. It got complicated, she explained, finding recipients for so many children's organs all at the same time. Usually, children that are strong and healthy don't end up in the hospital to donate organs.

Additionally, often the individuals who need a donor are older so they need larger organs. (Although I challenge their judgement on the size of Sawyer's heart, I think it was big enough to keep any adult alive, I'm just saying . . .) For us, this process just meant more time and we were tired. We had children at home who needed us to begin the process of understanding life without their brother. We needed to have this ordeal over with and to go home and shower and start to process an entirely new life. But the typical twenty-four-hour shift for Kate had come and gone and the recipients for all the organs had not been found. "You guys can go home, we know you have children at home who need you. We will call you with any news, we promise."

Leave? They said we could leave? How could we leave Sawyer—even if it was just his body—at the hospital alone? They'd call us? No. We were not leaving. "Sometimes we see parents who leave and then come back once during our shift, if that," said one of the nurses. "It's just too hard to stay." Jack and I discussed it and made our choice. We knew there was no right or wrong decision, there just aren't in these circumstances. Any parent, or person in this position, needs to do what they need to do to survive and the world needs to give everyone a little grace with whatever decision people make in challenging times. For us, we decided we could barely walk out of the room, much less the hospital, knowing we would be surrendering final moments with Sawyer. Then we spoke to Grayson.

Grayson called us the most during our time in the hospital. Wanting to know when we were coming home, he would call and check in often. We couldn't give him the answer he wanted, the answer we wanted, which was that we were on our way home. He'd called again and wanted to know when we were coming home. Originally, after Grayson said his goodbyes, we had told him it was only going to be another twenty-four hours and we would be home. Grayson had called to tell us it had been twenty-four hours. He wanted to know if we were on our way home. Our hearts collapsed yet again. It is a miracle of its own that each time our hearts collapsed over those five days that they eventually started beating again. Our judgment of "other parents" and their reasons for leaving the bedside smacked us in the face. Sure, some parents left the hospital because they were self-ish, but I would like to offer my totally unqualified opinion to say that is a small percentage. Rather, many more from the nurse's stories left because they had other children at home, sleeping on the floor of their siblings' room, hysterical that their world would never be the same. Someone had to comfort those children. Of course parents left, they had their own grief to deal with and no support system. Parents left for any number of reasons and we would learn many of them, but we would not stand in judgment of them again. Not of those parents, or of any parents faced with medical decisions for their child that (most likely) they, too, were ill prepared to make.

Jack and I discussed it and decided he would travel the 45 minutes home from the hospital to check on the children, shower, grab some comfort items, and return for the second twenty-four-hour shift to close out the organ donation process. Guilt plagues me over this as well. Guilt that I couldn't muster the strength to go home and strengthen my living children, because I needed to spend time with my child who had died, but whose warm tiny fingers and beating heart tricked me into thinking he was with me a little longer.

Jack came back from the house to report things were sad there, but the children were remaining strong and understood our need to stick it out with Sawyer until the very, very end. And then we met our second case worker, Nick. Jolly Old St. Nick, Jack called him, which was ironic because he was the opposite of Kate and her bubbly personality. He was quiet and pale and reminded me of the adult Pokémon players I saw when I went to tournaments with Grayson. He wore a gray sweatshirt over his scrubs and he didn't speak much. He was all about his job and he took it very seriously. He talked about how many of the procedures around organ donation you see on television and in the movies aren't accurate to the real-life process. But the one part that is the same is that last-minute helicopter ride of everyone getting to the hospital to gather the organs. As Sawyer would only have one final surgery for the recovery of his gifts, everything had to be lined up and everyone in attendance at once which meant a lot of phone calls once recipients were found and a lot of waiting on our part. And of course, more tests.

During these 48 hours we spent with Sawyer, we cried a lot, but we also laughed a lot and talked a lot. We talked to him as though he were still with us. We coached him along and reminded his little body to stay strong. At this point Jack and I had both moved into the bed with him. We even watched a couple episodes of Storage Wars, one of his favorite shows—a show we knew would require little emotional investment on our part and provide the distraction we desperately needed. We listened to music and took turns sobbing over his warm yet distant little body. It was so torturous. And yet I cherish those moments. I held both ultimate despair and joy at the same time as I downloaded a song I had heard and loved, "I Will Follow You," by Toulouse. I listened to it on repeat with him over and over again and pleaded for him to forgive me for not being a better mom, begged him to visit our family and remain a part of our lives in new and unknown ways, and sobbed over all the things I would never get to see him accomplish or participate in. The first twenty-four hours, amidst the surgeries and roller coaster of events, was hectic. The time with him waiting for his final surgery to donate his organs was sacred.

There are so many feelings and moments from that time we will never be able to share with the world or even our children because of their sacredness. While it meant our other children were required to bear this burden in the immediate aftermath without Jack or me to hold them, it was a time I now look back on as a gift. At the time the waiting and the continual delays were heavy, but I knew even as I was living them, they were something I would always be grateful to have been given.

In a surprise to us all, more delays meant more time at the hospital and yet a third twenty-four-hour case worker coming on board. Sam was our final case worker and he, like Kate and Nick before him, was exactly who we needed at that time. He was a large man, taller than Jack who is 6'4". He was loud and I remember he wore a braided belt with his purple Polo shirt tucked in. He declared we were closing in on all our recipients and would be able to make preparations for Sawyer's final surgery. Nick had been the one to deliver the disappointing news that only six of Sawyer's organs had found new life instead of the eight we were originally hoping to be placed.

After tagging Nick out, Sam persisted in trying to place the remainder of Sawyer's gifts. Sam was the one who came in to announce the last two organs were going to be placed and everyone was on their way. We were so grateful to have the opportunity for Sawyer to provide as many gifts as possible. Some transplant teams were fairly local, but others were flying in from across the country to retrieve Sawyer's gifts and the surgery had been scheduled. There it was, the news of a 6 p.m. Sunday night surgery, placed in our lap. It was a strange relief. Originally, three days earlier, when we thought the surgery would be on Friday, we told the case worker we were going to sit through the surgery and not leave until it was completed. She told us it could easily be a thirteen-hour surgery and we said we didn't care, we were not leaving until Sawyer was finished with his superhero task. If he could last, so could we. As I have mentioned, a lot changes as trauma unfolds and tragedy mounts, and that was true for us again. Things were deteriorating quickly at home with the children and we knew we needed to get to them as quickly as possible so we shifted our plan and decided we would say our final, *final* goodbyes and leave the hospital when Sawyer was taken to surgery. We knew it would then be time for us to turn our sights on the living.

But we still had a couple hours before that time. Those final hours, those final moments, are both fuzzy and clear in my memory. Together, though, those memories paint a picture to me of extreme love and ultimate sacrifice. It was in those final moments before the surgery, though, that we were given one of the treasures of this experience. The man who was to perform Sawyer's final surgery came into our room in the PICU. He too was a large man, as tall as Jack, and he wore a Hard Rock Café pendant on a leather chain around his neck. At first glance I wondered about the man who would place my sweet son's heart in his hands. He walked up to us and reached his hands out to give us a group hug. He said, "You can call me Brother Vaughn."

Did you know that there are about three million members of The Church of Jesus Christ of Latter-day Saints in the state of Utah? That's about 66% of the population. Did you know that in Virginia there are about 100,000 members of that Church? That's about 1% of the population. Ending up with a doctor who is a Latter-day Saint in Utah isn't odd, but to have a doctor who was a member of our church walk into our PICU room in the middle of central Virginia was a huge moment for us. We had been visited by our regional church leadership, a group of individuals responsible for congregations in the geographical area in which we lived. During our wait with Sawyer, they had come and done what they could to comfort us. Our direct church leader from our tiny congregation had been with us in the hospital since we had arrived days earlier and offered prayers, comfort, and blessings on our behalf. He brought the presence of the Spirit to us in the hospital. But to have this final doctor be someone of our faith, someone who believed Sawyer was where *we believed* he was, brought something powerful to us in that room at that moment.

Jack is a hugger. (Me, not so much.) But when Ty Vaughn said, "You can call me Brother Vaughn," Jack embraced him indeed as a brother. I acquiesced to the hug. (You should know I have since become more of a hugger.) They brought me into the embrace and we had a long group hug. Jack said to Ty, "You smell so good, like clean laundry." Huh?! We were in a strange place at the worst moment of our lives but we also had only changed and showered once in the hospital room which, needless to say, wasn't filled with lavish amenities. Ty laughed. We asked how he knew we were Latter-day Saints and he said one of our regional leaders, Brooks Baltich, had called him and told him he knew Ty worked on cases like Sawyer's. Baltich said, "I know you can't tell me if you are on their case or not, but if you are, you should know that Sawyer and his family are members of our church."

We asked Ty to say a prayer and he did. We asked him to say a prayer in the operating room. We asked him to love Sawyer in that cold isolated place like he was his own child. We asked a lot of him. We also asked him to bring us back a picture we wanted to send into the operating room with Sawyer.

When my sister, Brittany, flew out from New Mexico to be with us and to say goodbye to Sawyer, she was in a rush. She had about a half of a day to get her four children situated and her stuff packed, not knowing how long she would be in Virginia. As she was leaving her room to head for the airport, there was a photo on her dresser given to her by one of the youth she worked with at church. She grabbed the photo and brought it with her to the hospital. It was a print of the painting by Frans Schwartz called "Agony in the Garden." As soon as she arrived at the hospital, she gave us the print and we taped it with medical tape to the end of Sawyer's bed. It was a reminder that Christ Himself was a man of grief. That even He needed angels to protect Him and bring Him peace and comfort in His time of need. It served, for us, as a Protector for Sawyer, as he went in and out of the room for tests and more tests as we waited for the transplant team to arrive. We wanted the painting to follow Sawyer into his final surgery and it did. We trusted Ty to treat our baby with love and respect in his final surgery and to bring us home that little 4x6 photocopy of a print with surgical tape across the top. He did. We keep it in a frame near our bedside. It will forever be a reminder of the sadness and grief we know we felt and we know the Savior felt and continues to feel with us as we grieve. It also serves as a reminder that we don't have to feel less than, or unfaithful, or unworthy when we grieve. Christ, who was perfect, was also real with real emotions, including sorrow. Getting that print back was paramount for us because of what it represented and because it was the last thing that was physically with our boy. It was a connection to Sawyer we needed.

Ty was a connection we needed and we didn't even know it at the time. What do you call the person who held your son's heart in his hands? Acquaintance? Friend? Brother? Family. We call him family. We will forever be grateful to Brooks for making the call and connection for us. We also acknowledge the tender mercies of our story, times where we felt the hand of the Lord intervening on our behalf. Sawyer died. Of course, I would have given my own last breath to have had him live, to have God intervene and save him. I don't know why He didn't. I won't know that until I speak with God Himself when I graduate from this life. I am not thrilled about not having all the pieces of the puzzle, but I rely on my faith to sustain me until I am shown the whole picture. Reflecting on that point, feeling a thin veil between this life and the next, I know there are things that happened over those several days Sawyer was in the hospital, where God inspired and prompted others to act and serve on His behalf. People did things to offer us strength, try and ease a small portion of our burden, and serve as the Hands of God. I have many more thoughts to share around issues of maintaining my faith, but I firmly believe having Ty Vaughn there for those final moments of Sawyer's time here on earth helped rescue my faith in God and in humanity when I needed it most. A sense that we were not alone.

And while I know this is not the case for everyone who suffers tragedy and ends up in a hospital, we were so blessed to have competent and compassionate staff working with us from the moment we arrived until the moment we left. I imagine not having either of those characteristics in the people who serve you and your loved one during tragic times would bring an additional gravity to the grief you experience. I am grateful that is something we did not have to add to our shoulders. I will forever say, and I will repeat again and again, that during the worst time of our life, we were surrounded by only the best people.

But I digress.

# Chapter 5

# *The Immediate Aftermath for Our Family*

## Blessing for the Brokenhearted

*There is no remedy for love but to love more.*

—Henry David Thoreau

Let us agree
for now
that we will not say
the breaking
makes us stronger
or that it is better
to have this pain
than to have done
without this love.

Let us promise
we will not
tell ourselves
time will heal
the wound,
when every day
our waking
opens it anew.

Perhaps for now
it can be enough
to simply marvel
at the mystery
of how a heart
so broken
can go on beating,
as if it were made
for precisely this—

as if it knows
the only cure for love
is more of it,

as if it sees
the heart's sole remedy
for breaking
is to love still,

as if it trusts
that its own
persistent pulse
is the rhythm
of a blessing
we cannot
begin to fathom
but will save us
nonetheless.

—Jan Richardson

Used by permission. "Blessing for the Brokenhearted" © Jan Richardson
from *The Cure for Sorrow: A Book of Blessings for Times of Grief.*
Orlando, FL: Wanton Gospeller Press.
janrichardson.com

THE FORTY-FIVE-MINUTE DRIVE HOME, WHICH SEEMED LIKE HOURS, finally ended in our driveway. About five minutes before we reached our house, we decided we needed to pull over. We were in shock and traumatized from the prior five days and from the encroaching reality of the fifteen thousand more days ahead of us we were going to have to live without Sawyer. We knew we needed one more release of our own emotions so we could go try to comfort and mourn with our children and extended family. It was late, dark, and cold, but Jack and I both got out of the car and walked in different directions. We screamed, yelled, cried, and screamed some more. We dried our tears, got back in the car, and drove the last five minutes home.

When we walked in the door that night, we were a mess, and we had a house full of people there to witness it. We walked in the front door because I couldn't bear to go through the garage with all of his clubs, balls, undoubtedly dirty socks and skateboards. But the second we walked through the front door, I was hit with the sight of his blue high-top Nike sneakers, carelessly kicked off and cast aside (no doubt in the middle of the night after coming home from San Diego that Wednesday). I declared to myself the moment I saw them there, that those shoes would never leave my front door. Wherever I move, no matter what my décor, those shoes will stay by my doorway until the day I die as a reminder to me of the fragility of life and of my sweet, sweet boy with big feet.

I remember being worried about how I was going to feel when I got home. I was worried that it would be too overwhelmingly sad, and I wondered if I was going to need to go and stay at a hotel. My house has always been filled with photographs of Sawyer, even more so now, but greater than the photographs were the memories: The banister bar he knocked out on multiple occasions. The bathroom he never hung his towel up in. The bedroom he left sandwich after sandwich after sandwich in (long story for another chapter). My bedroom where he constantly hid under the bed to jump out and scare the crap out of me. The kitchen where we tried to make sushi and failed miserably. The dining room table. Oh that big, ugly, falling apart dining room table. We shared so many meals together, so many laughs there. We played countless game after game after game. We danced, oh how we danced around that table.

I didn't know if I was going to be able to relive it all and immerse myself in it all. I had told Jack in the hospital in a moment of panic, "We are going to have to move. Far away and soon." I went straight to my room and cried for a minute and then composed myself to the best of my ability. I had to; I had my three other children waiting for me. They needed me. I needed them. But we all needed space too. It was a strange time and none of us knew how to handle the situation or ourselves. We didn't know how to start, but we knew we needed to start with Grayson.

This is where the time line gets complicated. Sawyer was rushed into the ER by ambulance Wednesday morning. Wednesday and Thursday were spent in various brain surgeries. During those days Grayson was in and out of the hospital with us. Finn was at school because it was his first semester of college. Sterling was four, so she stayed home with a friend of the family instead of coming to the hospital those first days. Wednesday mid-day, when we realized things were not going to turn around and how seriously grave things were looking, we had a friend drive out and pick-up Grayson from school. Grayson had heard from friends that Sawyer had gotten hurt, but none of the children, and almost none of the staff, had any idea of the extent of his condition.

Grayson often heard through the childhood grapevine that Sawyer had been hurt. Classic Sawyer. Even if it didn't land him in a cast or Urgent Care, Sawyer was often engaged in outrageous stunts that landed him in the nurse's office. Hearing that his brother had left the school in an ambulance was a bit of a startle for Grayson, but nothing beyond his scope of understanding. Grayson later told me that he figured Sawyer had just gotten hurt in PE. It was Sawyer's thing. I remember vacillating at the hospital about whether or not Grayson should come up. Our angel friend, Melissa, was also the school nurse, had driven me in her van behind the ambulance. She stayed with us the entire time we were in the hospital no matter how often we told her we were fine and she could leave. Melissa said, "I think you need to get Grayson up here." We didn't want Grayson coming up to see Sawyer in that state and surely not to say goodbye, but Melissa knew what we couldn't accept. Even if Sawyer did make it through, he would not be our Sawyer. He would not be the brother Grayson had shaped and loved and nurtured and tortured the prior ten years. Grayson needed to be there.

So, we brought him up. He sat with us in that tiny family waiting room while we prayed and hoped and cried and prayed some more. Funny, the things that stand out in a time of crisis. I can't tell you the name of the doctor who did Sawyer's final brain surgery or the doctor who told us Sawyer was not going to survive. I can remember kneeling at the bedside begging that same doctor to go through every last detail over and over again, but I cannot remember his name. I remember Grayson eating Jello and making such a mess of it in the waiting room that I was almost embarrassed. I remember the sandwich from Panera that Grayson ate and saved the tomato for me. I remember he was wearing his donkey piñata button up shirt. I remember thinking that before that moment, I hadn't seen Grayson cry in a while.

Grayson had a burden to bear during all of this that none of his siblings had to endure. He was there during all the waiting. There during the decisions. There during the immediate trauma. It is something I will always be sad he had to endure at the young and naïve age of thirteen. Though it is something that bonded us in a way I am not sure anything else could.

Grayson lost his best friend and his brother. He has his own guilt about the type of brother he felt he could or should have been. He was thirteen and Sawyer ten. Of course there were rivalries and annoyances. It would have been strange if there hadn't been. But wholly, they were friends who talked for hours into the night. Friends who bonded over being uprooted from the home they'd known their whole lives, Radford since Sawyer was born, to Amelia where Sawyer died. Friends who shared friends and shared experiences because they were so close in age. Friends who went to the same school, who played for hours in the pool together, who jumped on the trampoline together, who nerded out on Pokémon together, who were slated to be on the same rec basketball team. I knew there was a whole other level of grieving Grayson was going to have to endure. Neither Sterling nor Finn would feel the loss the same way.

Grayson wanted to sleep in his own bed Wednesday night, and we totally understood. Another friend took him home from the hospital, but of course he was going to an empty house with only memories and fear to keep him company. My mom and stepdad lived three hours away, but at the time my mother was in Utah for the passing of her father (again, another chapter because that was its own thing). My stepdad wasn't usually the caregiver but as soon as he got the call from my mother, he was in the car and at our house just in time for Grayson to get home. It was a tender mercy to have him there to watch over Grayson and Sterling, who was also heading home from another friend's house. I will always be grateful the children were able to be in their own home, in their own beds, while all of those terrible strange things were happening around them. But at the same time, I will always be sad about how I was so consumed with the events at the hospital that Grayson dealt with everything essentially alone. I like to think that Sawyer visited him in spirit in those moments because it was Grayson who needed him most. We were there with his physical body and I hope Grayson had the company of his spirit during those impossible days.

More people flew in and more people were at our house as Thursday approached and we knew we were going to have to say goodbye to Sawyer. Finn and my mother had gotten flights in, as had my younger sisters and my aunt, who is more like an older sister to me. Jack's parents and my stepmother and father had also made it to Virginia. We had an army of people in the waiting room rotating in and out, but Grayson was in and out the most up until he said his goodbyes. We knew Friday was the day they were going to pronounce him as legally gone in order to start the clock on the organ recovery process. It is still difficult for me to type the word "dead." It feels so cold and morbid and uncouth. It feels mean, somehow, rather than just a statement of fact. There is a new power in that word for me. We asked friends and extended family to begin saying their goodbyes Thursday late afternoon.

Sawyer had a close friend who lived up the street from us. They were the first people we met when we moved to Amelia. We'd only lived there a few days when Lucas and his dad came up to the house dressed in their Boy Scout gear, fundraising for their troop. As a family of Eagle Scouts with Jack and Finn both having earned this award, and Grayson working towards his, we were drawn to their cause. We said we'd buy whatever they were selling. "Boston Butts." "Boston what? Did you say butts?" Sawyer and Grayson were laughing hysterically in the other room as I signed us up and wrote our check. We're not big meat eaters, so we didn't exactly know what we were signing up for, but we were sympathetic to the cause. From that day forward, Lucas was at the house often, or Grayson and Sawyer were at Lucas's house. They all enjoyed playing together, but Sawyer and Lucas really hit it off. They were both on the outrageous side, and Grayson could only handle so much of that. In spite of the four-year age difference, those two were bosom buddies. We had asked Melissa to call Lucas's mother and let her know what was happening. Their entire family came to the hospital and gave Sawyer and our family love and support we needed. I will forever be grateful to Lucas's parents for bringing him up to the hospital to say goodbye.

I think about that decision as a parent, about whether or not to expose your teenager to such overwhelming pain and sadness. I wonder if I would have made the same decision and, heaven forbid, the circumstances be in reverse, would I have let Sawyer go say good-bye. I hope I would. There was power in the company of those who knew and loved Sawyer being there to bid him farewell and thank him for being a part of their lives. My children were going to have to endure the pain and sadness, but in that moment, I realized there would be so many other children who would also have to endure this sadness with us because they loved Sawyer too.

He was loveable. I have said it before. This wasn't just our devastation. Sawyer's absence was going to be a strand of thread in the fabric of so many other people's lives as well. Everyone who knew Sawyer, or who had children who knew Sawyer, were going to have to discuss life and death and sadness and grief to their children in those next several days. I felt sad and sorry for all those parents, as well as for us. All of our other friends, coworkers, and family said their goodbyes at the hospital and left. Other than Jack and I, on that Thursday night, Sterling, Finn, and Grayson were the last to say their final words to Sawyer face-to-face here in mortality.

No parent. No sibling. No person. No child should ever have to look at another child hooked up to all of those machines and tubes, head wrapped and rewrapped, and whisper their enduring thoughts of love and friendship. Yet we asked each of our remaining children to do just that. We let them each whisper their final words and leave the PICU. Grayson physically signed Sawyer's hand with a marker, as if he were sending one last piece of himself with his brother. Grayson used that same Sharpie to trace Sawyer's hand on the Charizard stuffed animal Sawyer had brought home from Mexico for Grayson— the one Sawyer hadn't had the chance to give him yet. A final high five, if you will. It was gut-wrenching. It broke my soul.

And yet it was tender. It was beautiful. It was ugly and beautiful at the same time. It was the beginning of the realization that two seemingly opposing emotions could be held in the same place. Sweet Sterling gave him a hug and said goodbye. I could see she was confused and filled with emotions she couldn't place or understand. Finn did the same, but with the weight of knowing exactly what he was saying and the implications. With those final acts of ultimate love and intimate exchanges, the children left to go home while Jack and I stayed. We told the children we would be home Friday night and asked them to leave the hospital without Sawyer, knowing they would never see him again.

I feel terrible for not being able to take them home myself that night, but I could not leave Sawyer until it was all over and done. I know the children rode home with various family members that night, and while I know they went home with people who also lost someone that day, none of them bore the same burden Finn, Gray, and Sterling bore. And no one would be able to mourn and console them the way Jack and I could as their parents, but we had to let others try. Sawyer, Jack, and I still had another long road to travel. Little did we know how long it would actually end up being.

One of the nights we were in the hospital waiting for the transplant to take place, we called to check on our children. Remember, we had repeatedly broken the promise to Grayson that we would be home soon. The phone rang and a family member answered.

"How's he doing?" we asked.

"Oh, he is fine. We just checked in on him. He is laying on the floor in Sawyer's room watching TV on his kindle."

"He is just lying on the floor?"

"Yeah, he said he wants to sleep there."

"On the floor?"

"Yeah, but he says he is fine."

A foreshadowing of the power grief and loneliness would inflict.

A new panic welled up in us. No. He was not fine. For ten years Grayson and Sawyer had shared a room and just two months prior, when Finn left for college, Grayson had moved into Finn's room. In that moment of agony, Grayson clearly wanted to be in Sawyer's room but didn't want to be on his bed. I imagined the emptiness stopping him from climbing in. We asked for someone to at least pull a mattress into the room so our child wasn't sleeping on the floor in his dying brother's room.

Finn, our eldest son, was in not just his first semester of college but his *first six weeks of college.* During high school he had vacillated on whether or not to leave directly after he graduated high school to go and do missionary work for our church, a standard practice for many youth. Or, instead, if he should complete a year of college and then head out to do missionary work. After some procedural changes in the way missionary work was handled, essentially the age of eligibility was lowered which meant he would have a choice—leave immediately after high school or wait and go later. He'd decided he would go right after high school graduation.

He stuck to that plan up until the last couple months of senior year, around May 2016. He started waffling and wasn't sure whether or not he wanted to leave for his mission right away. In the end, he felt impressed to go to school for a year first. We were all a little surprised but since it was his life, we followed his lead. A couple months after Sawyer died, our friend Kate sent us a card and it read, "I'm grateful for the tender mercy of Finn not being on his mission yet, so you can mourn and remember together." There it was again, another punch to my gut. I hadn't even considered that yet! She was totally right, and I had a mini panic attack thinking Finn could have been halfway around the world when this happened. Thankfully, he wasn't. But he was all the way across the country in school and he wanted to return to see Sawyer and say goodbye.

Most of his professors were amazing, but he struggled to get one of his professors to understand the magnitude of what was happening. Finn wanted to return to school the week in between when Sawyer died and his Celebration of Life. If that were to happen, he was working on a tight schedule and needed to book his flight and leave Saturday or Sunday. We were still at the hospital dealing with everything there and yet we were also trying to help make decisions with Finn that would ultimately impact his entire academic career.

Finn has always been a "family-first" child and we have always relied on his maturity and sensitivity, but we were torn. He wanted to go back. We wanted him to stay. We prayed about it. We consulted family about it. We prayed more. Eventually we asked him to stay. We didn't just want him here, we needed him here. Grayson needed him here. Sterling needed him here. We, as his parents, needed him here. In the end we left it up to him, but he did decide to stay, even though I know it was a decision he made based on what was best for our family, not for him. I will be eternally grateful to have had him here during that week. But it was another reminder that the grief and stress we were under wasn't happening in a vacuum and it would be our task over the next days, weeks, months, and years to juggle it all.

And poor sweet Sterling. She didn't know what to do or how to respond or what to make of all the people coming in and out, Sawyer at the hospital not coming home, Mom and Dad gone, and then Mom and Dad coming home with a subsequent cloud of sadness hanging over our home. It all had to have been confusing for her four-year-old person. In fact, we know it was, based on things she said and did. It was terrible. We tried talking to her about heaven but knew she didn't understand. Honestly, the palliative care nurse worked with her a lot and I don't even know what exactly she was told. We could not be there for her and had to rely on the support system around us to guide her through those terrible moments.

It takes time to organize seven transplant teams from around the country, and with our variety of special circumstances, it took even longer than expected. I mentioned earlier that our original plan was to stay at the hospital until the end of the organ recovery surgery, to say our goodbyes at that time, and then leave. The final surgery didn't even end up starting until Sunday around 8 p.m. Remember, Sawyer had been rushed to the hospital Wednesday morning. All day Sunday as we could hear things deteriorating at home with everyone, most specifically whenever we talked with Grayson, we knew we had to leave Sawyer at the beginning of his final surgery. We would have to say our goodbyes earlier than planned (understatement of the century) so we could get home to our children left behind, our children who needed a mom and a dad to help them navigate the terrible grief and deep sorrow that was overtaking them. The sorrow that was overtaking us all.

# Chapter 6

# *The Public Denial of My Private Grief*

*"I walked a mile with Pleasure;*
*She chatted all the way;*
*but left me none the wiser*
*For all she had to say.*

*I walked a mile with Sorrow*
*And ne'er a word said she;*
*But, oh! The things I learned from her,*
*When Sorrow walked with me."*

—*Robert Browning Hamilton*

AT THE TIME OF SAWYER'S DEATH, JACK WAS THE SUPERINTENDENT of Public Schools in a small rural county in Amelia, Virginia. His acceptance of this promotion was the reason we moved three hours from where we had lived for fifteen years prior, a short two and a half years before Sawyer died. In Amelia, we were without the extensive support network we worked so hard to establish during the fifteen years we lived and raised our children in Southwest Virginia. Even as I write the previous sentence it sounds laced with accusation, but it is just a fact. A fact important to the story. When we moved to Amelia, we pulled our oldest son Finn out of the Governor's School in which he had worked so hard to gain one of the three coveted spots. We pulled Grayson away from the group of friends he'd known, the group of friends who loved him and gave him the freedom to express himself as an individual. Sawyer was pulled away from the opportunity to have his dad as his principal, something the other boys had both experienced and loved. We also pulled Sawyer away from his own network and comfort zone. Of course, Sterling was pulled along with us, but being so little, she didn't really know what was happening.

When we moved, we did so somewhat unexpectedly. It was supposed to be Jack's interview year. At the bidding of a very supportive boss, he started applying for jobs he felt were somewhat out of his league and definitely out of his comfort zone at the time. He was finishing his PhD and while he had a lot of experience in related fields, he had not physically worked in a central office, a fact we assumed would bar him from final offers. The interview year yielded quite a bit of success and he was down to one of two final candidates in three different localities. Mid-spring, we sat down as The Six Family to discuss what this success would mean for each family member. (Sawyer coined the phrase *The Six Family* to mean the whole family. We were often all going in different directions and it got confusing. These two would go to band practice, these four would go to soccer. One day we mentioned going somewhere and he wanted to know who exactly would be going. "The Six Family, or just some of us?" It stuck.) I worked part-time for the court system and wasn't sure I would be able to telecommute and keep my job. Finn might lose his spot at the Governor's School in Radford if it wasn't transferable. Grayson would be starting middle school at an entirely new location with no known friends. Sawyer would not have Dad checking in on him as the administrator of his school, something he'd been looking forward to since preschool. All of them would lose daily access to their friends and church family with whom they'd grown up. All of us would be leaving the assurance of having extended family close by. We had open and honest discussions. Several of them involved lots of tears, but not from Sawyer. Sawyer was ready to move. "I always wanted to move to a new house!" Sawyer exclaimed when we told him our final decision. He repeated his excitement often during our transition, which helped ease our concern for his adjustment. While reluctant, everyone eventually was on board and recognized the real opportunity it would be for Jack, and later came to see it as an opportunity for all of us.

We knew the move would also impact the way we as a family interacted with the public and the community. Growing up, Jack had repeatedly been an ecclesiastical leader at church. So our children had already listened to the "Represent yourself well when you leave this house" speech a thousand times. There was going to be a new level of scrutiny for us all, with Jack being in the public eye so much and the children being in "his" schools. Not to mention, Amelia was a small town and small towns have a heartbeat all of their own. What one person knows, everyone knows. What one sees, all see. Radford, the town we were leaving, was small. But nothing would have prepared us for the eyes watching and reporting everything we did from the second we set foot in Amelia.

To give you a sense of the watchful eye, I'll tell you about the night we drove the three hours to Amelia to watch Jack get sworn in as superintendent. It was before we had moved up there and we stayed in the county for maybe two hours. We left late the same night and drove home to allow the children to attend school the next day. The very next morning, Jack got a call. It was from a school board member and owner of the local newspaper. "I saw the bumper sticker on your car," she said. The bumper sticker read: *Mormons for Obama*. "I think you should remove it before you come back." To this day, I am not sure if her concern was over the Mormons part, or the Obama part. I imagine it was both.

The local newspaper became my nemesis. Okay, maybe nemesis is too harsh a word, but it was definitely the bane of my existence. Okay, still too harsh? Fine. It was a pain in my *patooky*. We didn't even subscribe to the local paper, but they sent it to us each week anyway. There was no avoiding the headlines when they covered "Dr. McKinley," something that happened more weeks than not. I knew it was going to be my struggle when in the first edition of the paper, instead of using my name Jaime Clemmer (I kept my maiden name and used it exclusively with rare exception) the paper referenced me as "Jaime McKinley, formerly Jaime Clemmer." The paper had managed to do what not even the Social Security Office had accomplished, it had renamed me. Photos of me or Jack doing things with the children at the schools often graced the pages of the newspaper and I didn't love it. In fact, it really bothered me, mostly because I felt like we needn't be "the example." Plus, I didn't like the idea that people I didn't know knew who I was. It was unsettling to me in my somewhat paranoid tendencies. Needless to say, the time the local paper reported to the entire community that we were on vacation in another country for two weeks set me off. In my mind, the article read, "Come, burglars, one and all. No one will be at the superintendent's home for two weeks, so break in early so it won't get noticed and the trail will go cold." Because of course, in a small town everyone knows where everyone else lives.

With time, I became more able to ignore the paper and the notion that we were living our life somewhat in the public eye. No, they weren't monitoring my electricity uses and no, I didn't stop taking my kids to school in the carpool lane in my pajamas, but I did shower before going out and I did take my "Mormons for Obama" bumper sticker off my van, per the helpful suggestion from the school board member. (The next election cycle I did put my LDS4HRC sticker up, but I had learned some things in the meantime.) Being in the public eye was usually inconsequential. I wasn't Taylor Swift and my comings and goings for the most part went unnoticed. That is, until my sweet boy was whisked away by ambulance from the local middle school in the middle of the school day. This tragedy, this hullabaloo in a small town, was not going to go unnoticed. And this is the part of the story where my grief was swallowed by rage.

We were in the middle of it all: three surgeries behind us, a terminal outcome in front of us, when we got the call. Jack had left the room to take a needed lap around the halls. We didn't leave the room much at all, spending every last moment with Sawyer we could. He saw one of the parents who had come to support us pacing up and down the hall looking even more stressed than she had been before. Jack approached her and asked what was wrong, other than the obvious. She said nothing, but Jack persisted. He does that. She said someone had called the Health Department and reported there was a virus killing the children in Amelia and it was at the schools and the Health Department needed to launch an immediate investigation!

A month prior to Sawyer's passing, there was a third grader also in our county who had died tragically and unexpectedly. It was sudden and horrible and caught everyone off guard and resembled Sawyer's death in those ways. But in only those ways. Sweet second-grader Isaac Guthrie died from leukemia. I say his name here because his mother and I have become friends in our common tragedy and every child who is buried deserves to have his or her name said and written as often as possible. Isaac had not manifested symptoms before he'd been diagnosed until he was sick one Friday with what his parents thought was a virus. His parents took him to the doctor and he underwent a rush of tests and procedures, but by Sunday Isaac had died. The disease had been diagnosed, the chemo started, and subsequently the chemo backfired, actually having the reverse effect (as it very rarely can) and spread the cancer so quickly that it killed young Isaac just three short days later. 72 hours. Almost the same amount of time Sawyer had been given from incident to passing. One fall day in 2016 each of these boys were fine, brilliant in fact. They were learning at school, playing at home, bringing life and light to their parents and friends and then suddenly, they were taken from us in very traumatic and unexpected ways, yet entirely unrelated.

But back to that moment. The moment the woman who called the Health Department made a split-second decision to listen to gossip and take matters into her own hands which stole final invaluable moments from my family with our son. Being the superintendent, Jack was starting to get emails and phone calls from reporters who wanted the scoop. The scoop. Any "scoop" is someone's life, someone's tragedy and on that day, it was ours.

Immediately, Jack went into protective father and livid boss mode, for someone had accused the school of not taking care of their own and the result now threatened to invade our privacy even more by sending reporters knocking on our hospital door. Pacing the halls resumed in full force. At this point we had moved into the bed with Sawyer, spending our last moments with him literally as closely as we could position ourselves. Jack was on the phone with lawyers and coworkers to get the story quashed, as it was not a story. Sawyer had a congenital condition, one that we had just learned about, but he hadn't even been pronounced dead yet, and the gossip vultures were swarming.

Their swarming led one woman into hysteria, to use alternative facts as the crumbly foundation for inciting panic, and, as a consequence, stole some of the finite moments we had left with Sawyer. Forgiveness becomes another thing altogether when you are talking about someone stealing final moments with your child, someone bringing a panic that your tragedy was going to be played out on the 7 p.m. news before you could tell all of your friends and family! Instead of having space and time to deal with the situation at hand, we were dealing with a selfish parent unwilling to wait and discover the truth.

Isn't that how gossip strikes though? Two children, two fatalities, in one small county of only about 13,000 people in a matter of less than a month. The parent who called the Health Department knew nothing. She had no knowledge. Yet she speculated, and heard snippets of information and conjecture, and took it upon herself to try and incite panic in the name of protection. Isn't that often the defense of those who act before thinking? In the meantime, she literally stole our privacy and some of our time with Sawyer to say goodbye. We spent that time fighting with reporters who eventually listened to reason, realized there was no story, and let it go, conversing with lawyers, and drafting public statements to abate concern. That was not the way we wanted to spend our time in the hospital with Sawyer. I try to think about all the ways I need Sawyer's death to sanctify me in the aftermath and this is one of them. In honor of Sawyer, I pray I will always remember to ask these questions before speaking, "Is it true? Is it kind? Is it necessary?" The heartache our family could have been spared if someone were willing to pause and ask those questions is immeasurable. People often ask, "How can we help?" One piece of advice I may offer after going through all of this, "Think before you speak and evaluate the consequences of what you say." But I have more to say on that in the chapter about how the English language failed me.

Needless to say, there was no Health Department inquiry, as there was no need. It did impact our approach to the situation, however. We felt we had to disclose to the world somewhat intimate details about Sawyer's passing. I would have much rather kept them personal and private. I remember drafting public statements from the hospital room and asking the peds nurses, the palliative care nurses, and anyone who was in the room listening to evaluate the statements we'd written. I recruited my friend Carol, a lawyer/editor with impeccable language skills, to help us draft the obituary, the public statements, and anything that anyone would read. We didn't trust our ability to formulate coherent sentences. Did our messages carry enough information? Were they personal yet panic squelching enough? Were they too personal or not personal enough?

Because of the scuttlebutt about the non-existing Health Department inquiry, every part of our narrative became important. What stupid things to have to juggle when you are literally in your son's death bed. Like I said, forgiveness becomes an entirely different, difficult game at certain points in your life. It doesn't change the impact of forgiving or the weight of not forgiving. For me, though, it is where some of my desire for sanctification came in, my intense desire to forgive so it didn't break what was left of me. Sister Neill F. Marriott says in her talk "Abiding in God and Repairing the Breach,"

> *It is now, with our mortal limitations, that the Father asks us to love when loving is most difficult, to serve when serving is inconvenient, to forgive when forgiving is soul stretching. How? How will we do it? We earnestly reach for Heavenly Father's help, in the name of his Son, and do things His way instead of pridefully asserting our own will.*

She didn't say, "Except when it is hard or you feel broken or if you are justified in your feelings of hurt and anger." She continued on to promise,

> *Independently forcing ourselves to have humility and trying to make ourselves love others is insincere and hollow, and it simply doesn't work. Our . . . pride creates a breach—or gap—between us and the font of all love, our Heavenly Father. Only the Savior's Atonement can cleanse us of our sins and close that gap or breach.*

I knew I would have to work on closing that gap and moving past hurt feelings in regards to several things surrounding Sawyer's death. But it was also in those quiet hours when I realized something about our tragedy. I was not going to be able to make this singularly "my" tragedy and keep to myself and hide in the back of the room, so to speak. It had been a very public death. Like it or not, this was going to be a public grieving.

Sawyer would want me to give you a corollary to the story, so I must even though it is totally irrelevant. Of course, it is never the stranger who incites riot, right? We quickly found out the name of the parent who stirred up all of the commotion with the Health Department. It was the mother of a boy who had been in Sawyer's class the previous two years. They were in Boy Scouts together. They weren't best friends but they were not enemies. It was the mother of the son who had a horrible flatulence/gas problem. A problem so terrible the teacher often had to stop tests and take the class out to recess to air out the room. The smell was so bad. The same angry mother of the boy who had eaten a jalapeño pepper that didn't sit well on his stomach and the mom blamed the children at Sawyer's lunch table. Here's the backstory—Sawyer and his friends loved anything spicy. One day, another boy brought a jar of jalapeños to lunch and they were all daring each other to eat one more than the next and Sawyer could eat a lot. Apparently, the one boy with the gas issue felt he had to eat one of the jalapenos to fit in, and it made his stomach sick. The mother called the teacher and insisted the children at the table had coerced the boy into eating a pepper. She insisted those at the table involved needed to be sternly addressed. I was called, the teacher and I chuckled and I promised to speak with Sawyer about his jalapeño habits and how they impacted those around him. Sawyer wasn't perfect. No child was, and to remember them in that way is a disservice to all of them. But as my new friend Amy (read, therapist) has told me repeatedly, the good, the bad, and the ugly are what made Sawyer who he was and it was that Sawyer that I love, not some whitewashed version of him and his childhood. So that's why I have to tell you the jalapeño story: context, I guess. Or maybe it is just an excuse to squeeze in one more Sawyer story.

# Chapter 7

## *The Celebration of Life*

WHEN IT CAME TIME TO PLAN A FUNERAL, NOTHING SEEMED RIGHT. He was too young, too full of life, too magical to sing dirges with his ten-year-old friends and church ladies all dressed in black with oversized hats. I knew we had to have a party. I almost instantly knew what I wanted it to look like as a whole, but the bits and pieces of planning the event to celebrate the life of one of my babies was overwhelming. If times and circumstances had been different, if Jack wasn't so well known in the community, I wondered if the Celebration would have looked the same. But I knew a private service wouldn't address the need for the community to participate in our mourning, and I felt obligated to concede. At first, it bothered me a little bit, and in the aftermath I realized it was a tremendous gift to have an army of mourners at my side. I started planning in the hospital. Planning meant I could make checklists, assign jobs, and distract myself from my terrible reality. In fact, I found that the week between Sawyer's death and The Celebration flew by. I didn't sleep, I ate very little, and I had a constant buzz in my brain as I obsessed over all the details. To this day I remember little of that week, which sits in harsh contrast to all of the distinct memories I have about our time in the hospital.

We had so many friends, colleagues, and neighbors step in as our busy bees and complete all the tasks we generated for them. We will continue to say how grateful we are to all the hands that did something to contribute to the beautiful community party we put together. Knowing I didn't want to be swallowed up in a room of black, this was put in Sawyer's obituary, *"The family asks that everyone dress casually for Sawyer's service. Cat T-shirts and vivid colors will honor Sawyer better than somber clothing."* We knew many of his friends would attend, and his friends were ten and eleven. We wanted a party-ish atmosphere, a Celebration. We said it and people listened. We saw cats riding dinosaurs eating pizza, we saw cats eating tacos (Sawyer's favorite food), we saw outer space cats, we saw it all. The children were excited about the crazy attire and showed up in full gear. Even the adults played along to make us smile. My serious-minded sister sported cosmic cat leggings ordered for her by her even more serious-minded engineering husband. People who were professionals about town wore metal placards around their neck with cats on them and T-shirts from Hot Topic. Only Sawyer could get my aunt, a walking J. Jill catalog, to wear a zombie cat T-shirt. He was like that, he was magical and he brought a smile to everyone, even in his passing.

The only exception we saw to the casual attire was from one of our beloved back fence neighbors, Mr. Walker. Mr. Walker and Sawyer had a fun relationship. When we first arrived in Amelia, we went and introduced ourselves. Mr. Walker was very good about remembering all of our names and calling us by them whenever we passed by or whenever we took a batch of his favorite pickles over. For some reason though, he initially switched the name "Sawyer" with the name "Stewart" and always called Sawyer, Stewart. We corrected him a couple of times to begin with, but then Sawyer said, "I don't care. I don't want to make him feel bad. He can call me Stewart. I kind of like it actually." Occasionally we too would call Sawyer, Stewart and we would all laugh. Mr. Walker said to us, "If you don't mind, you all can wear your T-shirts, but I will be wearing my best suit to honor my boy." And he did. And we love him for it.

Part of our angst about the Celebration, other than its mere existence, was who would officiate the event. We didn't want it to be a religious funeral service, but it was a chance to share our beliefs. As superintendent, Jack has had many opportunities to share our religious affiliation with those in our community. However, because of our important belief in the separation of church and state, he kept the nature of his beliefs to himself in public settings. This wasn't just another work meeting though, this was to celebrate Sawyer and our life together not just here on this earth, but our life with him in the eternities. After all, a huge part of our mourning and our coping is integrally tied to our belief that families are forever and that we will see Sawyer again. The conundrum. We decided we needed to have someone from our church to lead the Celebration as a secular event and we would hold a separate ceremony for just our family. However, while it was an event for "the public" we also knew it would need to be someone who could communicate some of our beliefs in a message of hope over the pulpit. We knew it had to be someone who knew Sawyer. That piece was critically important.

When Jack was first appointed the leader of our church congregation in Radford, he had been serving for two weeks and he got a phone call. Someone in the area had died who had not attended with our congregation but who was on the church roster. The extended family were not members of our faith, but in order to honor the wishes of their mother, the family of the deceased wanted Jack to do "whatever you do at your church." When Jack inquired about hymns to be sung or messages to be shared, they would repeatedly reply, "Do whatever you usually do, however and whatever that looks like." I think because it was his first major issue to deal with as a leader, funeral services throughout his tenure as leader were even more important to him than they might have been inherently. And during his five-year stint as the leader of our congregation, he conducted several funerals. Once, after the service of a gentleman from the ward (congregation), another elderly lady came up to Jack and said, "I hope you are still around when I die because that was a lovely service. You knew [the congregant] and we could feel your love for him. I want that feeling at my funeral." As we were planning Sawyer's Celebration, her sentiments stung in a way I never wanted to feel, but were suddenly entirely accurate and pressing. I wanted someone who didn't just love Sawyer, but who knew him. We had recently moved to Amelia, and we were still feeling those growing pains. I knew I wanted someone conducting the event who had known Sawyer long enough to really know him. It came to me: the leader of our congregation who succeeded Jack, Richard Fisher. He had been a family friend for years, had served together at church with Jack, had worked as a teacher in Jack's school when Jack was principal. He had even coached Sawyer in his favorite sport, soccer. It could only be him.

How do you call someone and say, "Hey. So, we need you to conduct a funeral service that isn't a funeral. It needs to be personal but not overly intimate. We need someone who knew and loved Sawyer but someone who can maintain composure throughout the service. We need the service to be filled with the light and hope of the gospel, doctrinally sound, but not overly preachy. So, what are you doing on Saturday?" How do you make that call? I can tell you how. You go out into the camper your neighbors brought over and parked in your driveway so you'd have extra space for houseguests, and you say exactly those words. You cry as you say them, but you say them. It was not a time for mincing words. It was a time to be clear and bossy. But we were having decision fatigue. We knew a lot of what we didn't want, but only some of what we did want. We had to throw control out the window, and for two control freaks, to say the loss of control was painful is an understatement. This was going to be the most important event of our lives and it needed to be perfect and we couldn't be in charge? It was another nightmare added to the bad haze of our lives at that point.

We had to trust. Trust God that He would inspire our friend. Trust our friend, who we knew was living close to God and would be able to receive inspiration. Trust everyone in attendance they would be accepting of the words and intentions in which they were being shared. Trust ourselves to know how to make one important decision and let all of the little decisions resulting from our initial decision just happen. Richard Fisher, our friend and former church leader, came and carried out our vision beyond any of our expectations. He brought both levity and the Spirit of Christ with him in equal measure. He relayed a message of hope. He also shared an amazing poem by Maya Angelou called "Life Doesn't Frighten Me," a poem which perfectly described Sawyer. But it also described how we would have to approach our new life without Sawyer. It was powerful.

*Shadows on the wall*
*Noises down the hall*
*Life doesn't frighten me at all*
*Bad dogs barking loud*
*Big ghosts in a cloud*
*Life doesn't frighten me at all*

*[ . . .]*

*I've got a magic charm*
*That I keep up my sleeve*
*I can walk the ocean floor*
*And never have to breathe.*

*Life doesn't frighten me at all*
*Not at all*
*Not at all.*

*Life doesn't frighten me at all.*

At the end of The Celebration, a gentleman from the community came over to us and said, "Thank you for ministering to our community in this way. It is something we all needed." People attended who grew up with Sawyer, and who grew up with me. People came who knew us intimately and spent literally every moment with us in the hospital. People came who I hadn't seen since high school. People came who had done missionary work with Jack back in the 1990s and he hadn't seen since. People came who lived nearby. People came who lived far away—some very far away. The media tried to come but Jack put his friends from work on the task of keeping them out, and they came through for us. People came who were friends of the family. People came who we hadn't seen in ages. People came who didn't even know we had a ten-year-old son. People came who didn't know Sawyer at all. People came who had taught Sawyer at some point. People came who were our friends. People came who were friends of our friends. People came. People flew in. People drove in. People stayed until the end.

At first, I was uncomfortable with how many people attended. I felt like it was a burden for them to travel so far and spend their entire Saturday with us by the time they'd travelled, stayed, and travelled home. But then there was something I didn't know until I was in the moment— I was scared. I was scared I was going to be there to mourn my sweet, sweet boy all alone. I was afraid I would be there to remember him, but no one else would be there to remember him with me. I was scared to mourn alone and thanks to the love and friendship of so many people, I didn't. I will draw strength every day of my life from the people who came for Sawyer and for my family that day.

From the time Jack was first a teacher, then a principal, and eventually an administrator, he has been touched by the death of students or immediate family members of students. He always made it a point to go to either the service, or the viewing, or the family home, depending on what he felt was appropriate. I never understood it. "How can you go to their house when you don't even know them? Don't you feel like you are intruding?" He always replied with some version of, "I just want them to know people care their loved one is gone and that they know people care they are hurting." He holds a high degree of empathy, something I have always loved about my husband. In fact, he was at the viewing for Isaac Guthrie a mere five weeks before Sawyer died. He came home shattered because he just wished there was something more he could do for the family, something to ease their burden. "I just can't imagine losing your child. What if that happened to us?" And suddenly we faced that exact nightmare.

As I reflect on this time of our very public grieving, I sometimes wonder how it might have been different if we hadn't lived a life that put us directly in the spotlight. Alas, that will never be for me to know. I'm not sure we were strong enough as a family to handle it alone. As part of the Celebration of Life, I wanted something for the children, Sawyer's friends, to be able to take from the "party," not just tears and memories. Sawyer's nickname was "Soy." When Jack first started calling him that, I hated it. Then Sterling came along and Sawyer actually started calling her "Stir-fry." Soy sauce and stir-fry, meant to be. I realized the name was going to stick, so I embraced it. Together as a family we sat around our living room trying to come up with an anagram for SOY that represented Sawyer. **S**trong. **O**utrageous. **Y**ou.

We had rainbow-colored bracelets made to hand out to those celebrating his life with us. This item wound up being quite popular, with the adults as well as the children. They went quickly.

At his one-year anniversary, we had another batch of bracelets made and gave them to several people who had asked because theirs was faded, broken, or those who hadn't gotten one originally and wanted one. We simply requested they wear their bracelets in circumstances that exemplified Sawyer (Strong, Outrageous, You) and send us a picture using the hashtag, #mysawyerbracelet. Posts from people in crazy places, under all sorts of difficult or unique circumstances, started popping up all over social media, my inbox, and my phone. They talked about being able to channel Sawyer's strength in hard times or bravery in scary times. My sister Summer is particularly good at eating tacos with her bracelet on and sharing it with me on the regular. It is ordinary, but she shows me she remembers, and I love it. I love Sawyer's memory being carted to all corners of the earth, on all sorts of adventures and having those experiences shared with me. I carry around the trauma of everything that happened to Sawyer. Strangers and loved ones alike carry his joyful memory around. In turn, that sense of remembering truly carried me through the one-year mark and beyond and has helped the way I combat some of my own trauma. I am routinely grateful for the love people share and hope more people will look for ways to share love and remembrance with those around them suffering any loss.

My friend's husband passed away a couple of months before Sawyer did. She has three teenage children at home and we have communicated more often in our grief. She too saw all the posts and pictures of #mysawyerbracelet and sent me a message:

*"I enjoy all the pictures and have so much respect and admiration for how you handle and approach life. I know it is rarely easy but the love between you and your family and friends is enviable. I guess the flip side is loving so much makes the loss greater, but for what it is worth, on some level I view you to be lucky to be surrounded by so much love. We did not have that and are struggling missing what we never had."*

Adding to that sentiment, my friend Casey has two children with cystic fibrosis. We met for breakfast one morning a couple weeks after Sawyer died. She has been told since her children were born that she will bury her children. How that must impact her parenting, her life, her daily routine, her prayers, her faith, her everything?! We talked about which was worse, not knowing your child was going to die and having him ripped from you in an instant, versus knowing your children will die and living with that heaviness daily. I vocalized concerns I had only processed in my head about how I would and wouldn't have parented Sawyer and what that would've meant. We concluded they are both equally terrible. I learned quickly that in child loss, for me, there is no such thing as "at least . . ." It is all just terrible. Anyway, during that breakfast, she said, "I know I won't be able to stand up in front of any size crowd when my children die, never mind the 500 people there at Sawyer's celebration. That is just too many people. I will hide away."

I wanted to hide away. I really did. But I didn't feel like I could. Whether it was some warped sense of obligation to Jack and his job, or to the community that had done, and would continue to do, so much for our family, or to Sawyer, or to myself, I don't know. Mostly I felt that because of the public nature of our life, and the profound impact Sawyer had on so many people in the short time we had been there, we needed that public celebration of his life to be the narrative, not the news article or the gossipy rumors. But whatever the reason, I am in the end profoundly grateful to have been able to share a teeny, tiny, microscopic blip of Sawyer's life with those around me. It makes me feel like he isn't forgotten and his life wasn't lived in vain.

I understand not everyone feels this way and privacy in grieving is their preference. Who knows, maybe it would've been mine in other circumstances. I've definitely had those moments too. I do know that at first I thought I was being denied my private grief. In the end I realized the blessing of having so many people know, be involved, and willing to share some measure of my sorrow and grief. In the name of mourning with those who mourn, having people stand with me, even if sometimes that meant leaving me alone, instead of leaving me and my family to stand alone in our grief, has been immeasurably powerful in our healing journey.

Since this manuscript was written, tragically, one of Casey's children, Sariah, died by suicide. Grief is complicated and terrible and the more I live, the more I learn how many people it actually plagues. And in spite of Casey's fear of being unable to speak, she stood at Sariah's funeral and was strong and brave and helped many people find a measure of healing.

# Chapter 8

## *The English Language Routinely Failed Me*

THE CELEBRATION ENDED, FAMILY LEFT TOWN, AND WE WERE LEFT to pick up the pieces of our lives. None of us wanted to go on living as we had, yet there were bills to be paid, jobs to be returned to, college semesters to be finished, and middle school to pick back up. Finn returned to BYU, Jack returned to his job, Sterling returned to preschool. Grayson took several more weeks off of school but he too eventually returned to his routine. While I sort of returned, I really didn't. I managed to keep everything around the house and in our lives running, albeit not as smoothly as it had been. But I hated to leave the house. The world continued to spin, but my little world seemed to be in a holding pattern.

Meet Robyn. Robyn's children attended the preschool Sterling attended and we were in a book group together. We didn't know each other well. We had never done anything together outside of book group and even in book group, while we seemed to share common interests and perspectives, we were not close. She had grown up in the area, as had her husband, and they had a tight circle of friends and four children. She didn't need new friends, but she was always friendly. When I had finally mustered the courage to start doing pickup and drop off again at the preschool, several weeks later (here I owe a debt of eternal gratitude to my mom and Brittany for sticking around and picking up the massive amounts of slack), Robyn was there. She didn't ask me how I was, she knew better. Robyn didn't ask why I was wearing sunglasses at 8 a.m. in the dark morning. Robyn got my email address from the LISTSERV and sent me a note. She got my phone number and texted me and told me she wanted to take me somewhere to get out. She said she could find us something to do unless I had something I wanted to get out and try.

Torn between my desire to never see anyone ever again and knowing the notion of becoming a true hermit was out of the question (only because of my spouse and children, otherwise I would've considered it quite viable), I said, "Why not, let's go get hot stone pedicures." I knew I wasn't myself because normally I would've said thank you and shrugged off the gesture, but I had agreed and even suggested an activity! I had never had a stone massage until right before Sawyer died. Jack and I had spent several days away together early in October, just weeks before Sawyer died (yet another guilt to overcome, being away when I could've been home with him in what I didn't know then were his last weeks on earth). His work conference agenda had sent me for the stone massage, and it was marvelous. It was an indulgence, for sure. Nothing I needed at the time, but something that now in my pain actually sounded somewhat appealing. A grief purchase. Add it to the list. It wasn't a new car, and short of that, Jack and I were being quite lenient on each other and our financial decisions.

Robyn did the research, found us a place nearby, picked me up and took us to breakfast and pedicures. She didn't make me do anything. The morning came for our outing, breakfast and a pedicure, and I almost bailed. There had been many calls and requests of me to "call if you want to talk or if you need anything," but I hadn't the strength or interest to reach out. But, somehow, I showered and went to breakfast. I rambled on about nothing at first but then I launched in. As I was talking to someone I didn't really know about intimate, personal, sacred pieces of my life, I realized I had desperately needed someone to talk to but hadn't been able to reach out to anyone. Robyn, having no experience with child loss, was simply there for me, tried to relate where she could and where she couldn't she would sit and listen in silence and say, "I don't even know what to say, there are no words . . ." And there weren't. There was power in her action.

Keep in mind I didn't know her well, but she seemed like "my people." At least more leaning in my direction than most of the other people I had met since my arrival to Amelia. She didn't ask me to "go back to where I had come from" (thanks, stranger dude at the five-year county planning meeting), she didn't ask me, "What does your husband have in store for the district in regards to gifted programming" (thanks, lady on the school field trip bus), and she didn't ask me, "Why don't you go to a church in Amelia, you'll never make friends if you don't go to a church in Amelia," (thanks, stranger at the library). Nor had she asked me to remove any of my political bumper stickers, so I call her a friend. Plus, she hadn't been at the hospital with us, she had a little distance from the situation, and I just needed to step outside both my house and my life for a little bit, so I decided not to bail.

Ever grateful for close friends, and even strangers who knew better than me, I was blessed for having gone out. I talked. She listened. I talked more, she listened more. I didn't have the right words to convey my feelings about so many things. I consider myself to have a decent vocabulary but I was experiencing emotions and living through things I could not describe. Robyn was patient with me as I over-explained and tried to conceptualize what I was trying to verbalize. When I asked a question, she gave me an answer. And not a pity-you-just-lost-your-son-I-will-tell-you-whatever-you-want-to-hear answer. A legit from-the-heart answer. My latest burden at the time of our breakfast was a decision we made very reluctantly to allow friends to post the crowdfunding site they had made for our medical expenses. We were struggling with the receiving end of charity. We had been given so much love and attention and assistance from friends and the community in the major tasks that had been dumped at our doorstep, and this seemed like too big an ask. I conveyed my concerns and guilt about the site and Robyn said what so many had already said, which was essentially, "Allow others to help you," but for some reason it finally stuck hearing her say it.

Several years prior, Robyn's house had burned down. Strangers and friends throughout the community and from her past had come to their aid, both physically and financially. She said at first the financial assistance made her uncomfortable. They had insurance, the house would be covered. But people needed a way to help. They couldn't all be there to unearth the rubble of what had been her home. They all couldn't host her family until the smoke damage subsided and her home was rebuilt. They couldn't all make meals or babysit children because many lived far away. They couldn't all be in her head and in her heart to help carry the burden that this fire had inflicted on her life and the life of her family. But they could send a check. A check to cover a meal out or a needed babysitter. A check for a pot or a pan that insurance wouldn't cover. A check to go buy something frivolous just to make her feel better in a moment of extreme sadness and pain. People could do that, and so could my friends and my family and people from my life. People I had met along the way these past forty years who loved me and cared for me and wanted to do something, anything, to lift my burden. I understood her. I understood what Amy and Carol, my friends who'd set up the site, had been trying to tell me. Carol texted me, "This is nothing to feel guilty about. This is you, accepting a little grace, a little love. I know it goes against your nature. But you guys have touched a lot of lives and it's okay to be on the receiving end."

I had this notion that if I were accepting financial help from people for Sawyer's medical bills then I should be scrimping and saving more so than usual, you know, buying generic Cheetos for the rest of my days. What a terrible perspective, heaping guilt onto myself based on judgmental assumptions I was making about friends who loved us and wanted to help. I am embarrassed and ashamed of how terrible I was at the other side of charity. My sister-in-law Jenny said it best and her sentiments reflect both my feelings and my new goal. "I'm practicing the fullness of charity this winter. Giving freely AND developing the art of receiving with grace. So much love and support have been showered on me, my family and it is sometimes an embarrassment of riches difficult to absorb. But receiving with grace is what's required to keep the circle of charity ever turning. Love and thanks to you all." (As an aside, she should be writing this book given her eloquence, but alas, it is my story and thus my burden to share, clunky narrator and all.)

Robyn also told me a great story the morning of our pedicure that illustrated a concept I'd been struggling with since I walked out of the hospital that terrible Sunday night. The English language had failed me and would continue to fail me in the wake of our tragedy. Robyn said, "After our home burned down, we had nothing. Especially nothing homemade. A group from a local church brought me a beautiful handmade quilt with lovely stitching and clearly a lot of love put into its creation. I was thrilled to have something in my home made with care and love and not just replaced from Target. Then I opened the card. I will never forget what the note said: 'We are sorry for your loss. But we are grateful Jesus DECIDED to save you and your family.' I kindly tucked the quilt away and tossed the card. People don't know what to say so they say horrible things and you just have to ignore it. Go with their intentions."

Whether it was because I couldn't identify the words to convey how I was feeling or whether it was because people were speaking words that I couldn't hear, either way I was feeling frustrated. Robyn, Carol, Jenny, and Amy conveyed love and compassion to me in words and deeds, actions I could not articulate for myself that I needed to hear or experience.

Words can help and heal, and words can cut and damage. This concept is not new. My grief amplified this notion in both directions, hurting and helping. Usually, it was when people didn't know what to say, they'd say stupid things. Platitudes and well-meaning quips that have not been thought out can actually have a reverse effect and impact many grievers in painful ways. I found that to be true for me anyway. Here are some stupid things I hated to hear when Sawyer died and why I hated them.

*"How are you doing?"*

Answer: Duh, our son just died. We aren't doing well. How about instead, tell me you will be around for me, or that I am in your thoughts, or you know it must be an impossible time. Something to acknowledge that we both know I am not doing well instead of making me say it out loud.

*"Call me if you need anything."*

Answer: I can't even remember my own phone number, never mind yours. And to be clear, I have *no* idea what I need. If you want to do something, do it, otherwise don't make *me* navigate how *you* cope with things. If you feel inspired to do something, do it, no apologies. If you don't feel like you know what to do, ask around. Look around. Or do nothing. But leave the burden off of the already burdened.

*"RIP, Sawyer."*

Answer: It feels like it should be an inscription on a Halloween decoration on someone's yard, not a sentiment for my aching soul. And while I truly believe Sawyer is in Peace, it does not make me feel better to hear you say that because his resting in peace does not mean I miss him any less. It might be a fun quip on a tombstone at Halloween but it isn't appropriate to me.

*"I hope you feel better soon, we want the old you back."*

Answer: Me too. I will, however, never be the same again. I am changed and I imagine this tragedy will continue to change me in ways I notice and don't notice and in ways I never imagined or desired. But hear me when I say I will never be the old me again, and I miss her too.

*"I can't believe <insert whichever famous person who died in 2016> died, what will we do without them?"*

Answer: Um, you will go on living, because while he/she was an icon to you, your world didn't revolve around them. Sawyer also died in 2016 and our world momentarily did stop at his death and we actually don't know what we will do without him.

*"I don't know how you are handling it. I know I wouldn't be able to deal with something like this. I think I would die too."*

Answer: The implication for this is really terrible. Play it out. What you are communicating is that the experience we just lived is so horrible you could not deal with it so you would . . . what? Not deal with it? How? What does that look like for you? For your children? For your spouse? Of course you would deal with it. Maybe not in the ways I am dealing with it, but suggesting it is so terrible I will never be the same is disheartening. Plus, it makes me feel like my grief is less somehow. That if I loved Sawyer as much as you loved your loved one who died I would have died? Killed myself? The comment veiled as a compliment to my strength comes across almost as an accusation, even if unintended.

*"I don't think you will ever get over this, I know I couldn't."*
Answer: I will never be okay with the fact that Sawyer left us way too soon and under terrible circumstances. When you say things like this, though, you are suggesting that I will feel as miserable now as I did that day. I could easily have forty more years to live. When you say this you are reminding me of the long tiring journey I have ahead of me, if I can survive it. Plus, you are robbing me of hope because I have to believe that cannot be true. I have to believe you too could do this, otherwise where do I turn? I have visited hell and I am climbing out of the hole. It is a different world I am emerging to, but I cannot believe God has delivered me to hell to let me languish there and never "get over it."

*"You are so strong."*
Answer: What? Because you don't see me weeping in the fetal position each morning, you think I am strong? If you did see me like that, would it make me weak? I would recommend reading the blog post "What Does it Mean to Be Strong in Grief?" by Eleanor Haley for a great explanation of this concept.

*"Saw your kids laughing. Looks like your kids are better!"*
Answer: So, since you don't spend two hours tucking them in at night because they are sad and crying about losing their brother, they are better to you? Because you didn't watch them turn their gaze and cry when the television talked about death, but now you see them laughing, they are healed? You have no idea as an outsider and that is okay. I don't expect you to know these things. But please, don't try to express your understanding on how others are feeling, especially if you only see them in passing or in limited environments. I understand you want to see them "healed" so they can go on living their lives.

Me too. But don't pat them on the head and brush off the long grief journey they have ahead of them simply because they are still children and still engage in childish behaviors.

*"God needed him more than you, I guess."*
Answer: *Just don't.*

And this one isn't an exact quote per se, but it still bothers me in similar fashion. There is a casual use of words and phrases associated with death and tragedy. Until Sawyer died, I was guilty of it myself. *"If I don't get this right, I am going to die." "If I can't get to the beach house soon it is going to kill me!"* Those rub me differently now that I know pain and grief and death in this way. It is surprising how often we hyperbolize phrases associated with death and tragedy when we are referring to trivial things. It makes those of us dealing with actual death and tragedy feel like you are minimizing our experience when you equate a bad haircut and wanting to die. Just something to ponder.

There are a few occasions when people have asked, "What do you want to hear? What is the best response or question people can offer if they want to say something?" Please hear me when I say this: Everyone is different and there isn't one right answer. Some of the things that set me off maybe wouldn't bother someone else grieving. I want to open up the conversation about grief, and that means sometimes we will say things wrong to someone who is grieving. Sometimes we will misstep. But if we are ignoring someone's pain, if we are so consumed with saying the wrong thing that we say nothing at all and never acknowledge death and grief and pain, we are doing everyone a disservice. My purpose in sharing my discomfort in these expressions is solely to get everyone thinking about what they say and what it might mean for the one to whom you are saying it. Knowing your audience, reading the room, and processing the implications of what you say and when you say it can go a long way. Find your own language and what feels right to the circumstance. For me, the clearly thought-out comments, the quick apologies when someone said something that hurt my feelings, and the acknowledgement of my pain helped me feel I wasn't invisible and my pain wasn't minimized.

I got a text one morning after a long night that said, "Shedding a tear for you today." It meant the world to me. No doubt I had shed some of my own the night before and as I arose that day. Sentiments expressing long-standing support carried me for miles. Sentiments that conveyed unconditional love were easier to receive than statements that conveyed judgment, even when others thought the judgment of the situation was positive, like, "Oh you are so strong." Well, consider—what choice do we have? For my family, we find comfort when people say something to the effect of, "There are no words, we just don't know what to say. But we love you and we are here for you." Jack and I have found this notion to be true over and over again.

I don't put this out there to intimidate you into thinking nothing you do can be right and nothing you say is appropriate when talking to someone struck by tragedy. It's just the opposite. People can and do say terribly insensitive things. What I have not decided is whether saying insensitive things is better or worse than saying nothing at all. I imagine for every circumstance and for every individual it is probably different. My two cents (technically three I guess) are 1) mean well, 2) speak out when moved, 3) but process what you say before you say it. And when there is a misstep, address it instead of letting it fester. If you don't know if there was a misstep but get a sense something has been taken the wrong way, broach the subject. My stepmother Nita, in referencing comments she makes about Sawyer's death, will say, "I am not sure if 'xyz' came across the right way the last time we spoke. If it didn't, will you please tell me so I know how to approach it next time."

While scant details had to be put out about what actually happened to Sawyer in the immediate aftermath, we remained pretty quiet about most things for a long time. To this day, there are details of the event so sacred to Jack and me and our family that we will never share them. Still, I knew the time would come when I would need to start speaking out more about not only what happened, but how we as a family were feeling about everything, what we needed, and our newfound desire to speak out about grief in general and about organ donation specifically. I knew it would start with baby steps.

One of the first people I reached out to outside our immediate network was a mom I didn't know from Sterling's preschool. I wanted to say things to a stranger. It was almost like I needed to practice saying things like "my son died." Like I needed to test out my new vocabulary on strangers so it wouldn't matter how it went down. It was odd, this mixed sense of the need for privacy versus the need for everyone to know how bad things were and how much I craved empathy and understanding.

November 17, 2016, less than a month after Sawyer died, I sent this email:

*Dear [Preschool Mom],*

*Not sure you will even see this but I wanted to share this story with you. I know you are a Thirty-One bag consultant so I wanted to tell you this . . . When we were in the hospital with Sawyer we were given a Ronald McDonald room. We didn't use it much because we wanted to be with Sawyer. In the room was nothing except a bed and chair and sheets and pillows and a Thirty-One bag. It was a small tote with a tag that said use it and that Thirty-One is a partner with Ronald McDonald. We had been at the hospital for days and we had rushed there with nothing except the clothes on our back. That said, we didn't use the bag because we didn't need it. As days passed and we realized Sawyer wouldn't be coming home with us, we started gathering his items and the things we would be keeping forever as our final mementos of our sweet boy. As we started gathering them, the hospital had those plastic clear patient bags. The thought of walking out of the hospital with the reminders of my dear boy, very intimate and personal things of Sawyer's, caused me to cry as I started to put them in the plastic bag. Then I remembered the Thirty-One bag in our Ronald McDonald room. I went in and grabbed it and filled it with his final things. Very important personal things. I walked out of the hospital leaving my sweet boy behind but I have a few treasures that I was able to carry out with dignity in that Thirty-One bag. It is still in my closet. One day I pray to have the strength to go through it. Until then it sits there. I'm so grateful it isn't sitting there in a clear plastic patient bag. Since I can't just thank "the company," I wanted to thank you. That's a cool and dignified service they provide and we are thankful for it. This is a personal story I share with you and ask that as a private story you keep it private. I just thought someone "at Thirty-One" should hear it. —Jaime Clemmer*

I shared intimate details, private thoughts, thoughts at the time I wondered if I would even be able to get out of my brain. I sobbed and sobbed as I typed. I cry as I re-read it. I waited for her response. I needed to hear her say something because I needed to know someone had been given a peek into our sadness. A day passed, two days, a week, two weeks, two months. Nothing. I never heard back. She never responded. Some of you may say, "Oh, she probably never got it." Maybe that is true. My take is that it was probably too painful, too personal. It was too much. This mom has children of her own, children who were happy and healthy and had their entire lives ahead of them. Why would she intentionally come into my space of sorrow and shock when it would only bring her sadness and sorrow? Before, would I have intentionally entered that space?

This is the message I want to get out to the world: Go and say something! Go and do something! Go into the sad spaces and sorrowful places. *Go!* Go there for people you know and love, go there for strangers, go there for people who you are mildly acquainted with, go for the person in the express check-out line at Target. Go there! You might have the words to save them, to rescue them from the dark hole they are falling into or have fallen into. You might be ignored or yelled at or brushed off. You might say the wrong thing, but try to avoid that by thinking about what you say before you say it. We may be totally prepared, have the exact right thing to say, and still it may not be received in the manner in which it was intended. Do not stop *going.* Try again. That is your burden to bear as the one who isn't in as much pain, I really believe that. There is an ebb and flow and you will be the one to offer and the one to accept at different times. If you are the one in a position of strength, you are the one to persistently check on the person in need. It is one of the many aspects of grief that is difficult to navigate. But that is why we need to talk about it more, and we need to talk about it more specifically.

You might be thinking, "What in the world do I even do? Or say?" In the next couple of chapters, I talk about what was helpful to me. Generally, anything that lets someone know you are thinking of them, thinking of their loved one, remembering that even though your world continues, you remember that theirs may be falling apart still and you acknowledge that and hold space for them in their grief. One thing that seems like something little but was a huge help to me was when friends would give me trigger warnings about movies, TV shows, or books that dealt with death, especially child loss. They weren't afraid to mention it to me and let me decide if it was something I wanted to bring into my life. I also had, and still have, people who will send me texts with quotes or messages of grief and resilience. Sometimes they come from people I don't even know well, but they say something to the effect of, "I saw this and it made me think of you. I hope you know you are not alone."

If you aren't in the exact moment of a crisis, you will think I am crazy, but it's a legit suggestion: practice things to say. Draft a couple of one-liners ahead of time to have in your pocket for situations when you see someone in distress. Ultimately though, bigger than the words you say are the way in which you say them. Use the English language to strengthen and bind you to others in their time of need rather than alienate them, inflict judgment, or impose your own beliefs. Have a couple of sentiments you can use that are thoughtful and well-intended and whatever it is, don't let it be *"How are you?"* or *"Are you okay?"* If someone is obviously distraught, they are clearly not well and not okay and they shouldn't have to lie to you. And above all, if you don't have the time, energy, or love to help the person, don't engage them out of obligation. They will know and you will make them feel like a burden which will only contribute to the distress.

I'm not that person, by the way. The one who reaches out to friends or strangers when the tears are flowing and the sadness oppresses the room. Well, I wasn't that person anyway. Prior to Sawyer's death, I would be the first to turn away or avert my gaze. In my mind I justified my cold shoulder as respect. "I am just giving them space. I wouldn't want someone to draw attention to me if I were sad and crying." My son Finn is that type of person—someone who reaches out to help a stranger—and it honestly made me uncomfortable. Or it did, before.

We had just moved to Amelia in 2014. Literally just moved there, as in, I had to put Food Lion (the only grocery store in town) into my GPS to grab some food for the family. Finn had come with me because we were going to check out phones that actually got service in our new locale, otherwise a trip to the grocery store would have been a hard pass for my teenager. We had both gone into the phone store together and then I ran in to get groceries and he waited in the car. I returned to the car and said, "I am going to call dad about the phones and then we can go back in and get signed up so just hang with me here in the car." I called Jack and was thick into the conversation about minutes and data and such when Finn got out of the car. I was talking to Jack but distracted by Finn's movements over to a car parked nearby. We had just moved here, he didn't know anyone. I watched him tap on the window, motion for her to roll it down and begin chatting. He was grinning ear to ear, definitely showing his "public smile." Finally, I told Jack, "Finn has left the car and is talking to a stranger. I need to hang up and see what is going on." As I started to get out of the car confused and concerned, Finn waved goodbye to the person he was speaking to and came back to the car. "What was that?" Finn, unfazed, said, "I saw that woman in her car crying pretty heavily and tapping her head against the steering wheel. I felt impressed to go and talk to her, so I did. She is having a rough time, some bad things are going on with her kids, and she just got more bad news. She said she was grateful I came over to check on her but that she would be fine. She thanked me and I left. So, are we getting the phones?" Uh, yeah, you can have a phone! And a Nobel Peace Prize on the side. And for all of you who think I actually bought my child a phone for being nice, to be clear, I didn't. He already had a phone; we just needed one that got service in the uninhabited (okay, maybe a tad extreme) countryside we found ourselves. I'm not that nice, remember? I was in shock and confused and my son taught me an important lesson that day. Most of the time you can't fix people or fix whatever is causing their grief. But you can, even if for a moment, step into it with them to remind them they are not alone. I was skeptical, but I filed the notion away in my mind.

Fast forward a year later and once again I was out with my family to celebrate something and it was late, so we turned to the only option available to us in our small town, McDonald's. We are a family who likes to celebrate and that usually means dessert of some sort. Our whole family was sitting around enjoying our cookies and "ice cream" when Grayson noticed a man crying at the table down from us. "Mom, should we do something?" He nudged me and I froze. Public space. Private emotions. Does not compute. I didn't know what to do or how to respond. So, I did what I often do when it comes to emotions I can't handle. I nudged Jack. Instantly, I mean, I could hardly finish my sentence and Jack was up and over at the table with the gentleman. They spoke, Jack gave him a hug and they walked to the counter. Turns out the man was extremely hungry, hadn't eaten in a while, and was desperate for food. Jack bought him a big dinner to get him through and made sure he had a place to go after dinner and came back to rejoin our family conversation as though he had simply stepped away to go to the bathroom or something. We finished our treat and headed home. I asked him about it when we got home. "How did you know what to say? Didn't you feel awkward approaching him?" I asked. "Of course I felt a little weird going up to him, but he was sad and no one was there to help him and so I just said what I would want someone to say to me. It wasn't a big deal."

But to me it was a big deal. I tend to be more reserved, more withdrawn emotionally, and I have learned something. I am selfish. I didn't feel comfortable approaching the man in McDonald's or the woman in the parking lot because I didn't know what to say. I didn't know what they would say. I didn't know how I would come across or how they would feel about me approaching them. Notice those sentences, they are consumed with "I." If someone is exceptionally happy or joyful it spreads, right? Someone smiles and you smile back. I think culturally we have this fear that the same is equally true about sadness and grief. Someone cries and feels miserable, it spreads. We cry, we feel miserable. Have you ever been in public and someone proposes? What happens? Everyone starts clapping and whistling and smiling, everyone wants a piece of the joy. Have you ever been in public and someone starts crying? What happens? Lots of different things but they usually revolve around averting glances, bowing heads, turning away, "giving them space," and the occasional approach or hug. While obviously respecting people and boundaries, I think we need to be a little more willing to share in the sadness of others and help them carry it, no matter how uncomfortable it might make us feel.

My neighbor, who had been keeping her distance after Sawyer died, approached me one day as I was burning things in the fire pit. She is a very private person and didn't want to impose, she said, plus she didn't know what to say, so she stayed away. I told her it was okay to do what she needed to cope herself, but her presence was important to me. Her coming over and acknowledging her inadequate words was more than enough. She said, "After I heard the news, I couldn't even look at your house when I drove by. It was too much, my pain, and it wasn't even my pain to have, but it was too much. I had promised Sawyer I would take him to Kings Dominion last summer. The summer days escaped me and suddenly it was time to go back to school and we hadn't gone. I intended to take him. I really, really did. But I didn't, and now I can't." I shared with her my feelings of guilt about all the things I intended to do with Sawyer and didn't and we bonded over missed opportunities. She then relayed the story of her own brother's death. I have learned, sadly, many people have an acutely personal story about death.

Her brother was seventeen and had just driven up from North Carolina to take her to her first semester at college in Virginia. He had dropped her off after helping her unpack and then headed home, as he was unable to afford a hotel that night and just wanted to get back. He was in a terrible car accident and did not survive. The guilt, the sadness, the loneliness, all of it was too much. She wanted to immediately travel home to be with family but her parents told her to stay in Virginia and go to classes for a few days. There was no room in their small North Carolina home to host all the out-of-town guests, and things were hectic and confusing and until she knew when the funeral was, her parents said it would be better for her to stay at school.

That night she didn't want to be alone. She didn't know anyone. She didn't have any friends yet. She had nowhere to go but knew she didn't want to be alone that night. She went out to a restaurant and stayed at the bar for hours. Several weeks later, after the funeral had come and gone, she had made friends, gotten a job, and was at work when a colleague approached her. The colleague said several people on campus had learned of her situation and had seen her out that night. They thought it was "insensitive to be out drinking the night your brother died." It had inhibited several of them from becoming workplace friends and had contributed to a negative opinion of her.

Wow! They had no idea. They didn't know what her staying home, alone, in a faraway place could have resulted in. They had no idea. She was honoring her parents' wishes to stay away until final plans had been made. They said things to her which impact her still, nearly sixty years later. They judged her according to their version of the story and hurt her deeply by conveying their judgment. How often do we do that? Judge a person or a situation or an experience based solely on our understanding of it, no matter how limited it might be and then communicate our judgment? Usually we don't mean to offend, but we say things that cut deep and are laden with judgment, even when we intend our communications to be benign. I am embarrassed to admit I engaged in that more often than I care to admit, and it is something I now work actively to avoid, saying things that could be interpreted as judgment in any form.

Another neighbor whom I love and adore, Mrs. Walker, came to check in on me just days after we had returned home from the hospital. She is older and has a definite opinion about things, but has always been good to me and my family. Whenever town gossip mounted about something Jack had or hadn't done "to" the school district, she was always the first to say to me, "Honey, don't you mind those pesky folks. The local paper and those who read it, they don't know anything. You worry about you and don't you mind their opinions. Just because those are the opinions we read about don't mean those are the opinions of everyone else. One loud voice isn't the voice of the whole community. You remember that, honey."

I have taken strength in the stories she and her husband have shared with me since we moved here. She has seen things and lived through things I never have nor will. As an African American couple in the south, she and her husband were faced with racist city workers when they moved in, racist county members when they needed permits, and racist neighbors, including the one who owned our house before us. Her husband once shared the story about the man who lived here prior to our owning the home. We learned this well after we'd moved in and established a relationship with them. Once they trusted us, they shared the story of our neighborhood racism. The man who lived here was a member of the KKK. He built a nine-foot fence around his home to block out the view of them and their home in his backyard. When they approached the city, they were met with dismissiveness and disregard. Eventually, invoking the neighborhood HOA policies, he was able to get the neighbor to take down his humongous nine-foot fence and replace it with a privacy six-foot fence.

Ah ha! I realized I'd just heard the explanation for the out-of-place four by four posts cut down at grass level we have to avoid whenever we mowed the back property line. I share this story to convey these are genuinely kind people who, having been truly offended, would still never intentionally offend others, especially those they loved. Especially us. They are people who have only the best of intentions. She came by the house one day and asked me, "How are you doing? I had to see for myself how you are doing. I am going to come check on you from time to time. You see my childhood friend and neighbor lost her son in a tragic accident when we were young moms. When her son died, she killed herself."

Gut. Punched. I know she had come to check on me to make sure I was surviving this seemingly impossible life event. I accepted her hug and sent her on her way. But as I sat and processed her words, all I could think was, "This is how bad things are. Others in my shoes committed suicide. Is she asking a legitimate question about whether or not I have tried to kill myself? Was the bar for my emotional stability so low that simply being alive was now the standard by which I judged how well I was doing? I am not prepared for the road ahead, this is too much." I know her intentions were only honorable and kind-hearted. She was my back fence neighbor, my friend. But my broken, sorrowed heart heard only this: "When other people experience what you have experienced, they killed themselves. This is bad and going to get worse. '' It felt like too much too soon and was not the counsel I needed at that time, mostly because I wasn't stable enough to hear it. Surely, it's not the message she intended me to hear, but when people are grieving, everything gets filtered through that grief lens, which makes auditing what and how we say things critically important.

Fast forward to November. I had a meltdown in the lobby at the Marriott in Virginia Beach. Sawyer died at the end of October, so Thanksgiving and Christmas were right around the corner and we were an absolute mess. We collectively decided we were not ready to celebrate Thanksgiving. We decided we would refer to it as "Thursday." We have always had a huge meal surrounded by friends and family for Thanksgiving and we knew that would be too much. We were also still struggling to be thankful for anything.

We chose to escape our memories and go spend a couple days at a hotel where we could do "Thursday" activities totally uncommon to us. We went to the beach. We mostly watched television and played on our various devices. We did drive the boardwalk to see the Christmas lights but that was sad in a whole new way. As we were driving through the light display, Sterling said, "These lights remind me of Sawyer." "How so?" I asked. "We would be having a lot of staring contests and he would stare at the red and I would stare at the green and we would try not to blink." I cried. I love hearing stories from Sterling. I love hearing stories from his friends. I love hearing stories from his brothers. I love hearing his name. But all of these words and stories hurt as I hear them, they hurt as they are spoken. There is no language that could convey these stories in a way that doesn't make me cry. But not hearing them, that would break me. I once read, "Hearing your name brings music to my ears and tears to my eyes," and it is entirely true. Anyway, we spent our days in seclusion and eventually had to return home for Monday responsibilities.

We had loitered in the lobby a lot that weekend. No one was there and the restaurant was always closed. Sterling had knocked over some hot chocolate one day and the receptionist had politely helped her get a fresh drink and clean the mess. We had sort of abdicated our typical manic parenting style for a more "laissez-faire" approach because we were in survival mode. The staff had been polite and mostly ignored us. I imagine for them they see rowdy kids and absentee parents more often than they'd like, but it wasn't my style and I started to cry. Nothing hysterical or panicked, just simple tears rolling down my cheeks. I got Sterling and her fresh cup of hot chocolate and we went upstairs.

It came time for us to check out. We had escaped the four sad walls of our own house in exchange for the sad walls of another place, but it was time to return. The woman at the counter, who was the same woman from the previous hot chocolate incident said, "Your daughter is so smart." They had been chatting, as Sterling will chat with anyone who is within earshot. Without thinking, I said what I always say, "She has three older brothers who have taught her well, and early." Sterling chimed in, "Yeah, except for Finn because he is at college and Sawyer because he is up in heaven now."

I started to weep and the woman said, "I'm so sorry." I shook my head, held up my hand to the woman to indicate it was okay, and spattered a couple of "It's okay, don't worry," type responses and we left. Jack pulled up to the curb in the van, having left Grayson and I the only witnesses to the exchange between Sterling and the employee. We started to load the van and the woman from the counter was suddenly at my car door. She asked if she could give me a hug and I nodded my head unable to speak. Grayson, tender himself having witnessed the event, avoided eye contact with everyone and got in the car quickly to cry privately. She told us she would keep us in her prayers and we drove off. Seeing we were all disturbed, Jack asked what happened. I relayed the scene and he of course teared up as well. Then we hear Sterling from her car seat say, "Did you know you can only watch Hello Kitty in Colorado?" Huh? What?! *Kids are so strange.* "How do you know that? Why do you think Coloradans are the only ones who get to enjoy Hello Kitty?" "Because Sawyer and I watched Hello Kitty in Colorado once [*true*] and he told me."

Jack told her in the car, "I like hearing stories about Sawyer." So, to change the mood I randomly asked, "What do you think Sawyer's favorite sport is?" (thinking the answer is going to be soccer or basketball) and Sterling chimes in, "Volleyball. I definitely think it is volleyball." We all laughed because while he may have played volleyball casually with us at the beach here or there, Sterling had sat through a million of Sawyer's soccer and basketball games, but nope, she thought volleyball. It made us laugh.

You can see the scattered nature of grief in this incident, especially for a four-year-old, but you can also read about the compassion of a total stranger. There are so many times people said things that have brought tears to my eyes, sometimes good tears which evoke love and memories. Sometimes people have said things that have been hurtful and confusing, and I cry wondering why someone would be so aloof, mean-spirited, or just thoughtless. Nonetheless, words have power. Especially in grief.

My final thoughts about language boil down to this: we aren't children. Sometimes the concept, "If you don't have anything nice to say, don't say anything at all" doesn't work. We never set out to say rude things to people who are grieving, but we can often, unintentionally, say things we do not think through. We are adults with complex human interactions that do not adhere to a recipe of "Match this situation with these words." Crafting something genuine to say may take thought but it is always worth the time. Maybe there are times no words speak with the most power. And sometimes just saying "I don't know what to say, but I love you and you are not alone," is the best thing you can say.

I remember being in a church class years ago and the woman giving the lesson harped on the notion that too many people get offended too easily and leave church forever. She said something to the effect of, "If someone says something you don't like or you don't agree with, ignore them. Don't take offense, people don't mean to be rude, they are usually well intentioned." She focused on the subject about the responsibility of the offended to overcome the offense the entire lesson. It's true. There is a place for forgiveness and assuming the best of people. I have said it before. But that does not mean there isn't an equal obligation we all have to try our very best to *not be offensive.* As the lesson was coming to a close, I had to speak out. (This should come as no surprise to you at this point. Cue the eye rolls from the folks in the back.)

At the time she spoke, I was thinking of when someone asked me how far along I was in my pregnancy and I told them I wasn't pregnant. I was just getting fat, but thanks for noticing. I offered the comment to the group attending the church lesson, "One thing we are forgetting in all of this is that we need to try and not be so offensive. We put such a burden on others to not take offense and to overcome that we at times use it as license to say whatever we think and whatever we feel. We don't worry about how our words will be perceived because, 'We didn't *mean* to be offensive.' We should make our first and every effort to try not to offend."

After that exchange years earlier, I regularly tried to think about the words I said and where I held my obligations, to be less offensive and take less offense. Back then, the offense was about my body image, a big deal but nothing that would plague my world view or impact my spiritual beliefs. Now I was encountering people who were saying things, well-intentioned comments no doubt, but that often hurt my feelings at the very core of my soul. I understand people don't mean to be offensive, but I think there are times people also don't try hard enough to not be offensive. This whole experience with Sawyer has turned me into more of a "slow to speak" sort of person. Before I always rushed to speak. I needed my opinion heard. Now I find greater need in evaluating whether or not what I have to say is really something that needs to be said. It's not to say I will never offend anyone. On the contrary. I am sure I will, but I will try harder to couch my words in kindness and follow up more quickly with an apology when I learn an offense has been taken.

My friend and her brother, Robyn's do-gooders, my neighbor at my front stoop, and everyone else who stopped me or called me or emailed me to share their perspective of how I should feel during this time, they all meant well. I don't fault them for their use of the English language and the way it impacted me or my friends. However, meaning well is not an excuse, an explanation maybe, but not an excuse for not showing compassion and caring for people with the language we speak. When we choose to approach people who are in the thick of their trial, whatever it may be, we need to think about what we say before we say it and consider the implications before we just let the words run out of our mouths. It can mean the difference between someone's burden being lightened and someone's burden pushing them to the brink.

# Chapter 9

## *The Hospitality of Grief*

WE COULD NOT BELIEVE THE OUTPOURING OF LOVE AND SUPPORT WE got from our community when Sawyer died. When we started to doubt God or His love for us, we would recall all of the ways people served God by way of our doorstep. When Sawyer died, we had only been in our small, not particularly keen on outsiders, tight-knit town for two-and-a-half years. The support network we had spent fifteen years establishing in Radford was three hours away. While many, many people from Radford stepped up and helped as they could from afar, when we needed immediate help (I call it first-aid help), a new network was quick to step into action. I am still flabbergasted at how many cards we received, how many meals were delivered, the thoughtful plants and flowers that were sent, and the many more ways people showed they cared. We got lots of help creating the PowerPoint of his life and adding the exact music we wanted when we wanted it to play. To everyone else it was background music, for us, it was in some ways the final summary of his life and every note was critical. People arranged for food at Sawyer's Celebration, which was awesome because Sawyer always asked whenever he had to go anywhere, "Will there be refreshments?" Yes, kiddo, we had refreshments for you. People provided scads of food for those we love who came out to honor Sawyer. We needed help drafting public statements and obituaries, and Carol was there to make sure every word was perfect and conveyed exactly our message. A complete stranger to me, but a friend of a friend named Tim Pakledinaz, drove three hours to record on video those who were too hesitant to share their Sawyer story publicly at his service. And so, so much more. The cold hard truth? There was nothing anyone could do to fix our situation. But watching people take over the mundane tasks consuming our life helped us feel their support and also helped us remember that God, who felt so far from us in our tragedy, was actually quite close.

Sometimes people now ask me, "I have a friend whose [insert any loved one here] just died. I never know what to say or what to do. So, what helped you the most so I can do that?" I wish I could tell you everything people did for us. Part of the humility for me comes in knowing I will never know all the things people did to ease our burdens. Consequently, I feel an enormous sense of gratitude that regularly brings me to tears. Katie Couric, upon surviving the passing of her husband years ago, said,

> *If you know them, intrude on their privacy by reaching out, even if they turn you away. If you don't know anyone who fits into this category, say a silent prayer for them, wish them strength and what Emily Dickinson described as 'the thing with feathers'—hope.*

She was specifically talking about surviving the holidays, but I think it is appropriate for all times when you know someone who is grieving. I also feel that even if you don't know someone, there are ways to respectfully invade their privacy by reaching out. I know people did for us and we were ever the stronger because of it. There were so many public, private, and even anonymous ways people served us. So, in the vein of sharing what helped us, I would offer my brief discussion of *Dos* and *Don'ts* for the bereaved. I know lots of lists are out there and I know everyone is different in their grief which is why listening to the still small voice in our hearts and acting accordingly is so important. That said, it isn't exhaustive, but here is a sweet and condensed version of my list.

# Things people did/brought that really helped:

## Action and Presence.

For me, one of the biggest gifts was the presence of people. It was difficult to navigate my mourning. I often heard the question "What can we do?" I didn't know what we needed, never mind how to ask for it. I couldn't tell someone, "Yes, I would like fried rice and Kleenex with lotion. Such gifts will make my mourning more purposeful and my burdens lighter." In fact, I found I suffered from decision fatigue quite easily. I had just spent the past week in hell making one terrible decision after the next over the worst five days of my life. To then be asked, "What can I do to help?" was a question I simply couldn't answer. The kind acts of service that just happened were blessings. The texts that came in saying, "We don't know what to say, but know you are on our minds," were a welcome pause in the tears of the day. The people who showed up with trash bags, cards, paper goods, and toilet paper for all the many unexpected but entirely necessary house guests, and even just a sorrowful look and hug were some of the knocks on the door that I appreciated most. Especially when they were not the last I ever heard from that person.

## Food.

Yes, I know I said earlier not to just drop off a casserole. Let me tell you a story that has nothing to do with me to try and clarify before I launch into my food talk. A friend once told me a story about an experience her mother in-law had. Her mother had broken both her arms and they were both in casts and her father-in-law worked all day. Her mother-in-law would be left alone for hours each day and was feeling quite lonely and rightfully so, a bit sorry for herself, unable to do the things she usually did. One day her mother-in-law heard a knock at the door. She yelled, "Hold on, I'm coming." As she slowly worked herself out of the chair, she was thrilled at the anticipation of a visitor. Slow to move she hollered, "I'm coming, just give me a second to get to the door." Upon arriving at the door, she took awhile to fiddle with the door to get it open because of her dual casts but could only get the door unlocked. She said, "The door is unlocked but I can't get it open. Come on in though." She waited and waited and no one came. Later that night when her husband got home, he brought a lasagna in from the front porch. All my friend's mother-in-law wanted was someone to cut through the loneliness of the day, not a casserole she wouldn't even be able to eat. (Ok, before all the naysayers jump in here and talk about all the scenarios that explain why the person didn't come in, don't miss my point. We should seek to serve others in the ways they need to be served, not in the ways it is easiest for us to serve them. That is all I am saying. Back to food.)

We were flooded with food. Southerners know that essential to surviving any period of mourning is to ensure bellies are full and freezers are stocked, and my community did just that. My sister had found an old purple composition notebook lying around and turned it into our Mourning Headquarters. Anything anyone needed to know about what was to happen at the Celebration, who had come to visit, flowers that had shown up, meals that had been delivered and by whom, appointments to be kept, phone numbers to be called, everything was in The Purple Book. As I went to look for something in preparation for the Celebration, I saw a page header entitled, "Inventory of Food in the Freezer." We had lists for everything. People brought a lot of food we didn't have to ask to receive. In the immediate, we loved the deli and vegetable trays, things we could all snack on (we had lots of visitors from out of the state and there aren't a lot of restaurants close by where we could grab food). Plus, smelling food cooking made me nauseous. I wasn't able to eat but other people needed to and not having my house smell like bacon or some other potent food was helpful. Breakfast items, those were awesome! Some food was heated, some frozen for later, and everything labeled. I have cooked for many years, I know how to heat a casserole, but somehow my mind wasn't working, or sometimes the teenager was putting food in the oven and didn't know what to do. Knowing what was under the aluminum foil before we cooked it, and knowing how to cook it, was perfect.

Sawyer died three days before Halloween, but we didn't get home from the hospital until the night before Halloween. My four-year-old wanted to go trick or treating. My older boys obviously did not. A friend invited Sterling to go along with their family and then they sent candy home for my older boys. The simple gesture meant the world to them immediately and more to me in the long run. Kid-friendly food was our favorite. While the adults liked everything, our children weren't having a lot of it. It was a stressful time, and the notion of comfort food became clearer than ever. Shalini, the wife of Jack's coworker who visited us in the hospital, made a huge Indian feast, which was beyond amazing. On top of this overflowing box of aromatic, home-made food, sat a Happy Meal for Sterling. He said, "My wife insisted I stop and get chicken nuggets for the little one." Perfection, everyone was satisfied. Now anytime I take a meal for grievers, I always include something kid-friendly, just in case.

People continued to bring food in occasionally long after it was "necessary" and well after I thought we needed it. I am almost embarrassed at how grateful I was for those meals, almost more so than the ones that came immediately. I will confess, cooking was quite difficult for me afterwards. The first time I tried to even pull dishes out to set the table for only the four of us, when just two months prior we were The Six Family, made me weep. Finn went back to college and we were left a small family of four and I couldn't adapt. Meal planning was sad. When I did muster the strength to cook, I always ended up with leftovers. I had trouble adapting my portions. Which meals did Sawyer like and Grayson not? Which of the condiments in the fridge were ones only Sawyer would use? It was all so painful. So, having a day out of the blue when a meal would just show up was amazing. Never having to ask was also amazing. I know if I had put the call out, meals would have shown up for days, but I didn't think I needed them. Others knew more of what I needed than I did.

## Learn when to ask and when to act.

My friend Karen performed this touching gesture for us the first Christmas after Sawyer died. It had only been two months at that point and we were a hot mess. Karen had taken action and pulled photographs off my Facebook page and had them printed in a calendar. They were mostly pictures of Sawyer, but they also included Sawyer with the rest of us as a family. Before she did it, she asked her friends at her card club. She talked it out with people and asked what they thought of her idea. Some were unsure, but one woman who was a widow said, "Do it. She will love it. It will probably make her cry, but she will love it." She wasn't sure when and how to give it to us. We had gone to see her and her husband Juergen for a brief evening while we were back in Radford for Christmas. She said, "I have something for you. It will probably make you cry. You don't have to open it here, you don't have to ever open it, but may I give it to you?" Honored, I took the gesture, unsure of what it was, and indeed it did make me cry and I did love it. I love that she had a generous thought and she acted on it instead of vacillating back and forth about doing something kind. But I also love that she asked others, specifically people who had known grief and death and would be able to offer her an insight she needed to approach me in my grief. The thoughtfulness that accompanied the question strengthened me.

## Show up, especially if you bring consumables.

I couldn't believe the stockpile we received of paper plates, plastic utensils, trash bags, and even toilet paper. It was brilliant. I have a smaller family, but Jack has eight brothers and sisters and their spouses and children flew in. While they didn't stay with us, they were at the house a lot of the time. Being surrounded by love and comfort and an army of people who loved Sawyer was critical in helping us survive this time. All of the products people brought in went to good use. Could any of them gone out and picked things up for us as we needed it? Of course. Having those supplies on hand meant family were around to perform other tasks like preparing for Sawyer's Celebration of Life, distracting my surviving children, cleaning my house, and simply sitting around telling stories about nothing but meant everything to me at that time. Those were gifts. Plus, having napkins for almost six months was awesome. Any little thing we didn't have to think about or restock or fret about not having was amazing.

## Offer time.

I was always surprised every time the door rang. "We don't know this many people," I kept saying. Turns out I didn't know that many people, but Jack did. And our children did. And those people loved and served me out of their love for my family. Finn's friends from high school stayed at our home during the Celebration because I had heard break-ins were prevalent during times of funerals. Unlikely? Yes. Did it bring me huge comfort not worrying about it? Of course. Sawyer's dear friend who came to the hospital to say goodbye just showed up one day and started mowing our lawn. Several administrators from around the region cleared their schedules and drove all the way out here to bring love and support for our family. None of them had met Sawyer. But they came, they told funny stories about random things and made us laugh. They didn't act like they were in a rush to leave, even though all of them had pressing schedules and long rides home. Staff from the schools spent long hours working to cover the extra responsibilities Jack's absence created and then *after* working long days would come by the house with books and toys for the children and meals for the family. Friends came and took our recycling and trash away for us. Time from others was spent doing our day-to-day tasks that needed to be done so we could have space and time to grieve. Give people the gift of your time by showing up and offering.

## Send thoughtful messages.

Our hallway for two years was lined with the cards people sent. People I know sent lovely cards expressing condolences and shock and love and concern. People I did not know who heard our story from a friend of a friend sent us cards. And everyone in between sent us a card. It was powerful. I couldn't even open them all each day as they arrived. We would open a couple and save a couple for the next day and the next day, more would arrive and we would repeat. I haven't had a lot of experience with death, particularly with the death of someone close to me. My paternal grandmother with whom I was not particularly close passed away just after Jack and I were married. It struck me as my "first death" but I wasn't acutely impacted by her loss. My maternal grandmother who served as a second mother to me my entire childhood had passed away several months before Sawyer died, but we had said our goodbyes the last time I visited and so while it was extremely sad when she died, it didn't change much of my day-to-day life. I had dealt with a lot of that grief already. The true impact of her death was felt the final time she and I said goodbye months earlier. In the past, when I heard of someone dying, I would go to my card stash and pull out whichever grief card was on top, write my thoughts and prayers to the grievers and send it along. I had no real understanding of the impact of grief and how many mourners are dragged down into the pits of despair, desperate for some light and comfort.

I know now that the cards matter. Many groups and individuals sent cards and every card mattered. There were many, though, where I could tell the sender spent time choosing the card, capturing the perfect image or the most compassionate and personal message and those cards saved me. I have mentioned it previously but again, knowing I wasn't alone in my sorrow and knowing I did not mourn Sawyer alone, truly that knowledge saved me. No more buying grief cards in bulk for me. Looking up an address, buying a card, and getting a stamp are easy ways to connect with people who you are close to and people you don't know. It is an easy gesture that can have a big impact.

## Express love with reminders.

Along with all of the cards, we also got packages. Each package contained something beautiful and beauty begets beauty. It seems odd, and I never would have thought of it myself, but people sent tokens to represent their love and my loss and I adored everything people sent. We got a simple ceramic heart with the phrase "Thinking of You." It rests on my bookshelf so every time I sit and read it, it reminds me that I am not far from the thoughts of my friends. A sign that read "Our family is a circle of strength and love" arrived from an acquaintance who had her own fair share of grief and understood a portion of my loss. This was powerful because I thought, "I knew her, but we didn't know each other well. And yet she still sent this lovely gift." Despite our brief connection, we now had a deeper connection and acknowledging that meant the world to me. A wooden painted sign with our new family motto, "Heartbroken, But Not Broken" arrived not long after all of the visitors had left us and we were trying to adjust to our new life. It hangs in our kitchen as a daily reminder that though we may feel it at times, we Are. Not. Broken. We got an angel figurine around Christmas time that will forever rest by Sawyer's stocking. So many more things came to us at a time we needed to be remembered and our gratitude brings me to tears as I think of the love people showered upon us. At the one-year mark of Sawyer's death, I went to lunch with my friend Jayne and told her I needed to find the rainbow and unicorn brigade to survive and a few days later a lapel pin of a rainbow and unicorn arrived at my door. I wore it all week and still pull it out on tough days. It was a little gesture that held a lot of power in the camaraderie it brought. Sending a small token can be quick and thoughtful and provide lasting memories that someone cares about you. It did for me anyway.

## When you can, share money.

I don't even want to say it, but it is true. The money people donated to us in our time of grief really saved us. People sent money and it made me uncomfortable. I've mentioned this before. In lieu of flowers, we asked people to donate to a scholarship fund in Sawyer's honor. We are able to generate enough to give scholarships for the years Sawyer would have remained in high school. It still gives us comfort to be able to share his love and life with strangers in that way.

The fact so many strangers and loved ones gave so much is overwhelming. I was more comfortable with these gifts, reasoning many people would've sent flowers anyway. But the giving didn't end there. Right before Christmas, we started to get the bills. Talk about overwhelming, those were overwhelming. Not to mention sad, and maddening. We were lucky enough to have insurance, but 20% of a *heckofalot* of money is still a *heckofalot* of money. Then there were the little things starting to appear on our charge card statements that were both direct and indirect expenses of death. The chargers we had to buy in the hospital because we just rushed there and ended up staying for days and needed to communicate with the outside world. The numerous trips to the food court during our hospital days. The door we had to buy for the office because we had turned it into a bedroom for Grayson who wouldn't return to the bedroom he shared with his deceased brother. The extra minutes and data we used on our cell phone plans. The plane tickets for Finn's last minute trip home and later return to college. The price of the urn we wanted for Sawyer. The litany of expenses mounted.

The actual cost of grief was expensive. But not just expensive, infuriating. The bills coming in revealed to me how angry I was about Sawyer's death. The money became something I could direct my anger at and I shared my anger with a friend. Mostly I had been sad and left the anger to Jack. I didn't like the anger and needed it to go away. After much soul searching and humility we did concede and allowed people to donate to help cover our portion of the bill. When our friends set up a crowdfunding page for us, we reached our limit within three days. We didn't want a penny more than our insurance was billing us for. Thankfully, our insurance had a maximum allowable expense because three brain surgeries were not cheap. The anxiety I felt over the degree to which people gave to help us out was beyond matched by the relief I felt over not having to lose my child and get stuck with the bill for his death.

## Did I mention money?

As his one-year mark approached, (I refuse to use the word anniversary, which technically doesn't require happiness by definition but definitely connotes celebration, which I am not doing), I had hoped the school would do something to remember Sawyer. Some people had talked about putting together a golf tournament to raise money for the scholarship fund and we were thrilled. But things fell through the cracks and the tournament didn't happen.

When we realized it wasn't coming to fruition as we had been told, I was almost in a panic about doing something in his honor. I reached out to the organization we used for the organ donation. They have an extensive support network for donor families and while they had reached out often, there wasn't anything I needed from them, so I mostly deleted the emails and tossed the letters when they arrived. With no golf tournament on the horizon, I reached out and asked if the organization had any connections to help me do a billboard for organ donation awareness in Sawyer's honor at his one-year mark. Yes, they did! I was thrilled. They sent me an application for a grant I could write and request funds. The woman I worked with was hopeful it would be funded, said it aligned perfectly with their education promotion campaign, and said to submit my application for review. I wrote up the grant and sent it along, hopeful. A couple of days later I got an email. "Unfortunately, I was unaware the grant applications are only for 501(c)3 applicants and families are ineligible to apply. My apologies." Curses! Again, my hopes for memorializing Sawyer in a public way had been dashed. I sat around for a few days, depressed nothing was happening to remember my boy, also exhausted from the grief, never mind the idea of a project involving tasks and energy. Then my depression again turned to anger. "Sawyer was taken from the school where his friends and teachers watched him in his last moments of life! Why isn't someone doing something or reaching out to me?!" I was self-absorbed and it turned to anger. Eventually the school did put together a memorial rose bush planting for him at the suggestion of a parent with a child in Sawyer's class and it was a beautiful ceremony.

Reflecting back, I realized the times I was angriest about everything were the times I was focused on myself. I do believe anger was a justified and rational response to losing my child, but I don't think it helped me. I know it didn't help me when I turned my anger towards other people. Even my sadness and sorrow contributed to my healing but for me personally I felt more at ease with my sadness than my anger. The grieving world talks about how sorrow starts to settle in your bones, and I found that to be true, but the anger did nothing for me. Anyway, in an attempt to distract myself, I got on social media and saw a clip about a father who lost his son in a car accident and he created a touching memorial space near the accident. The business it was near, after years of his attention and caretaking of the space, reached out to him and helped him create a more permanent structure. What struck me from the clip was how the father took action. He didn't sit at his pity party and wait for someone to come to his rescue and honor his son, he honored his son himself. Lightning bolt moment. I was Sawyer's mother. I could create something. That's when I realized I was committed to the billboard and would take the project on myself.

Turns out, billboards are expensive and that is when I turned to Sawyer's army. Again, in a short amount of time, people sent me donations to cover the cost of his billboard for three months! If I had enough time, I could've saved the money for it myself, but having so many people invested did two things. It helped me achieve my last-minute goal of getting the billboard up in time for his one-year mark, which I do believe, and was told by numerous people, was a service for the community in and of itself. It also again brought to my mind and my heart the active love, care, and concern my network of people had for me and my family. A year later when the prayers and meals and "first aid" assistance had mostly subsided, but we still needed help honoring Sawyer, people sprang into action immediately. It brought power and more healing to my broken heart.

## Send thoughts and prayers, not ironically, and not just the actual phrase.

"Thoughts and prayers" is a phrase that gets tossed around a lot. Lately I've heard a lot of criticism around it too. Offering sincere thoughts and heartfelt prayers on the behalf of someone else can be powerful. Our entire family felt the power of the collective praying for us in those early days, even months after Sawyer died. I believe those prayers kept us getting out of bed every morning, kept us from not making terrible choices that would've brought more pain, buoyed us as we were sinking into the depths of our grief. I truly believe that. Those prayers followed up by action and presence had the most powerful impact though.

One of the ways I felt the results of those prayers came in the form of numbness and even a tiny sliver of peace. I know that sounds strange, numbness. I believe there are times in our lives when God has to speak to us in different ways than usual and this was true for me. I felt my numbness was a gift from God, truly. (Yes, I also know physical shock was a component of that as well.) I do not think I could've handled everything otherwise. Still, I think the criticism of the phrase "thoughts and prayers" can be valid because sometimes it is said and heard in a vacuum. Regularly there are no accompanying actions and sometimes there are not even prayers to coincide with the well-meaning sentiment. Have you ever been guilty of saying, "You're in my prayers," and then never following up with an actual prayer? I have. And it isn't because I didn't intend to, it is because I got busy, I didn't make it a priority, and because I didn't stop right then and there to say the prayer, leaving my mind as quickly as I'd expressed it. It sounded good. It sounded like the right thing to say, and I meant to . . . Maybe it is just me, but don't worry, I've made amends. If I say it, I follow up with it and include someone in my prayers. If I don't think I can or will, I don't say it.

One of the most consistent comforts I have felt is when people say, "I'll be thinking about you" and then they actually let me know they were. A short text, a message on social media, an email or voicemail, "We told a story about Sawyer today," "I think of you as I listen to my music on the Sabbath," or "During the children's program at church today we thought of you and how hard it must be missing Sawyer." Thoughts and prayers, when followed up with actual thoughts and prayers and actions, are what brought power to that phrase for me in our time of need.

## Remembrances, in any and every form.

Long after the initial round of condolences, I had people who stepped in and helped me remember I was not grieving alone. Parents of Sawyer's friends would send photos of their children wearing their SOY bracelet while traveling across the country, at the beach, watching the Superbowl, or just going to a school dance. My friends would do the same. One of Finn's friends from freshman year, Miranda, was there to watch the aftermath of Finn both navigating his first year at college and his first year without Sawyer. She beautifully, wholly, responded to the call to remember. She didn't even know Sawyer, barely knew Finn, and really didn't know me. But still she wore her Sawyer bracelet everywhere. When one would wear down and break, she would ask for another one. Several people did. For years after Sawyer's death, Miranda would honor and remember him in every exotic country she went to and every outrageous thing she would do. It warms my heart in a way I can't even explain every time she, or anyone, would send me a text or message that they were remembering my sweet, gone, but not forgotten, Sawyer.

Even seemingly little things can have a stirring effect on my day and change the way I am processing my emotions. My friend Beth had a son who played soccer with Grayson many years ago. We didn't really know each other but became more acquainted over Facebook once we had moved from Radford. Every time she has the letters to do so in her online word game, she spells out the word "Soy" and sends me a screenshot. It is something little I presume on her part (except for those who play word games, you know the value of surrendering an "s") but something so touching to me. It brightens my day every time.

Some outrageous things are little, some things are big, but anytime someone asks me about Sawyer, remembers Sawyer, or acknowledges him as still part of our family, they are giving me the absolute best gift they can give me. Like when people share with me that they tried a new food for the first time in Sawyer's honor. Or when they wear the bracelet into surgery to give them strength, or at a job interview to give them confidence. I love those moments and the way they create a legacy for Sawyer. I also am amazed when the big gestures come as well. Sawyer, as you'll remember, was only in the sixth grade for a couple of months. But during those months he made some amazing friends who have done a lot to remember and honor Sawyer. One in particular brings me tears on the regular.

His friend Landon has started driving race cars. His mother reached out to me and asked if we would mind if Landon put the image of Sawyer's organ donation billboard on his race car. We were honored. Every time he races (and he both races and wins, a lot) he mentions how Sawyer rides right alongside of him, right near his head. The angel wings he races on are of my sweet angel. And I know Sawyer's spirit is screaming with glee during every adventure Landon is taking him on. (He's probably also doing some sort of "nanny-nanny boo-boo" face at everyone who doesn't get such a cool front row seat to the action!)

· · · · · · · · · · · · · · · · · ·

I want to emphasize *all* of the things, both material and immaterial, we received at this terrible time in our life, and that have served us in our healing journey in the extended years afterwards. We still turn to the wall of cards or the memories of people showing up when we are having a hard day and those memories and reminders carry us into the next day. Truly. I know not everyone who is grieving gets this sort of support. That is a big part of why I am telling my story to the world. People in times of suffering and tragedy usually need more than *just* a casserole, even though we loved and devoured the casseroles we got. Offer more of yourself to those who are mourning. Whether it is a text, call, note, visit, or token (or maybe even a race car, just spit balling here). We needed a multi-prong approach to our first aid and we didn't even know it. We definitely didn't know what it would look like. But when we see it, it buoys us and builds us up. We were blessed beyond measure. I would love to be able to one day be in a position to buoy others. Until then, I hope you will be the strength for those around you who need it.

# Here are some things I am begging you NOT to do . . .

## Speak without thinking.

In the hospital after the first surgery, several people close to us had heard what was going on and had come to support us. Particularly one close friend and her husband had left work to join us and bring us food and sit with Grayson who, as you know, was in shock. In passing she said, "They should have life-flighted Sawyer to the hospital. Why didn't they life-flight him?" Gut punch. We were in shock ourselves and trying to grapple with everything happening. At this point we still had hope he could possibly recover, even if he wasn't going to be himself, and we were struggling trying to reconcile that reality. We hadn't even thought about life-flight or second guessing any of the decisions we or any of the medical staff had made up to that point. There hadn't been time. Out of nowhere this bomb had been laid in our lap and with it a load of guilt and embarrassment and terror came with it. Could we have saved his life if we'd pushed for life-flight? We didn't know at that point what was happening. The paramedics didn't know either. We had all acted in a way we thought appropriate and here a dear friend, speaking more out of shock I am sure, was questioning what we had done or not done to intervene in saving Sawyer. We were heartbroken. Of course we asked the doctors and the neurologist in the aftermath, asking if that could have made the difference in Sawyer living and dying and they responded with a resounding "*No!*" Once the episode (the rupture of the AVM) began at the middle school, which presented with a seizure, the event was underway and there was nothing that could have been done from that point forward. This stupid AVM did exactly what it set out to do from the beginning and no life-flight or quick thinking or medicine or anything could have stopped it from taking Sawyer from us. It was then we realized Judgment was upon us. From the way we handled the first moment of this event up until today when people still judge us in our grieving, people look from the outside in and try to impose their judgment on how we did and are handling everything. So, at the top of my list of things to not do, don't make comments on how someone should/could handle things in times of trial, trauma, and tragedy. The person who made this comment about the helicopter is still a dear friend, she didn't mean ill, but her words still fell powerfully on us at a time we needed nothing but positivity.

## Did I mention speaking without thinking?

It was our first summer without Sawyer but we had survived, barely. It was tough during the school year, but the days kept us occupied and the evenings and nights were the most painful times. The summer brought entire unoccupied days reminding us that we weren't at the pool as a family, we hadn't gone to the beach and swam in the ocean as a family, we hadn't been to the amusement park together, and the boys hadn't bonded together in mutiny over the summer reading schedule which was more devoid of screen time than any of them liked. It had been rough, but we had survived. I went to a Back-to-School play group and ran into a friend. "How was your summer?" she asked, innocently enough, but it was thoughtless. Had she paused and thought about who she was talking to, she might have had a sense of how we were doing. Tired of putting on a smile and saying, "Fine!" to everyone about everything I said, "Actually, it has been pretty tough and the children especially have had a rough time." And then she said the words that blazed my soul. "Oh, yeah? Still? Hm. Uh. Yeah. Sure. Of course."

*Still.* Yep. Still. It was the only word that mattered. Stunned, I said something like, "Yeah, summer isn't as fun when your best friend has died." She followed it with something like, "Oh, yeah, well that makes sense," and we parted ways. Again, I know her intentions were to quickly (emphasis, on quickly) assess how we were doing, but genuine concern coupled with a better understanding of grief would have known a quick pass at the door wasn't the place to acknowledge me in my grief in that way. It might have looked something like, "Summer has probably been hard for you all. I've been thinking of you." Or it could've even been any moment prior to that exchange since I hadn't seen her in several months, maybe a text or email to check in. Or it could have just been a hug or nod and the simple but profound, "We were thinking of you this difficult summer."

At the beach one-year, our nephew Haden, who always vacations with us, had the most obnoxious phrase, "Silence is golden, but duct tape is silver." He thought it was hilarious 1) because he was in middle school but 2) because all the little(er) children were non-stop chatter boxes, Sawyer at the top of the list. While I hate the phrase and the implicit violence it implied (I can feel my older boys rolling their eyes as I type that sentence), I have thought about it a lot since. He was implying the priceless nature of silence and the only way to get it with these little ones was perhaps by using, shall we say, *external motivation*. Sometimes, if you don't have the right words and you can't or won't take the time to come up with the right words, silence may be the best option. You don't have to ignore someone. You can still acknowledge their presence, even their pain, without saying a word.

## Keep your opinions to yourself unless asked. And even then, tread lightly.

(Are you sensing a theme?) Spring break was approaching and as a family, we were feeling trapped. Trapped by our responsibilities, by the four walls we shared with Sawyer, by yet another celebration we would not be sharing with Sawyer, and by the people who gave us knowing glances and pitiful looks. We needed to escape. We have always loved to travel as a family. Usually it was long weekends away, often to a beach, but it could be anywhere. Traveling now was hard because we were not whole, but traveling felt good because it took us to new places where there were no memories of Sawyer to trigger our sorrow. The literature and the families we had met who'd experienced a similar tragedy said traveling was the only way to survive the first year, and we took it to heart. We left to go anywhere, anytime we could. Spring break meant a week away, so we started watching for airline tickets. We booked the first cheap tickets we could find, Italy. Within 24 hours, our credit card agency contacted us and told us they flagged the expense as fraudulent and they rejected the charge. We didn't typically buy international airfare, so go figure. When we called the airline company, they wouldn't honor the price and it had sky-rocketed. The whole point was a cheap ticket, so we abandoned Italy and kept watching. One afternoon, tickets to Paris popped up cheaper than we usually paid to visit family in California, so we jumped. We spent the week in Paris.

Grieving is exhausting and difficult. Grieving in Paris was exhausting, but less difficult. We could neglect our memories and abandon our sorrows as we tried new foods, went new places, explored new things. We had zero expectations and operated under the guiding principle, "When it's not fun, we're done." It totally worked. Even though we were on Netflix at times or playing a board game, being on Netflix in Paris or playing SCRABBLE in Paris helped. Obviously. I wish a trip like that for everyone who is grieving. I wish a trip like that for us more often, but alas it isn't realistic. But I am grateful we were able to make it happen. Not everyone gets such a gift. However, for the weeks just prior to the trip, I felt intense guilt.

People I loved and trusted made remarks of varying shades of, "Don't you feel guilty spending money on such an extravagant trip when people paid your hospital bills?" Or another one was, "Don't you think people will be wondering if the money they gave you for the scholarship fund paid for your trip to Paris?" Blow. To. The. Heart. Well, I hadn't thought that, until you said those things. Would people really think we misused their money? Would they really question our financial need and regret helping or judge us for accepting their help? I know the money for the scholarship fund sits in the bank and will until those seven years have passed and the money has all been gifted. I also am keenly aware if it were not for people helping us with our bills, we never would have been able to make this important trip happen. This was the first trip we took as the Four Family. It was the first trip we established memories distinct to our life as a foursome, going somewhere Sawyer had never been nor ever wanted to go. It was the trip we took to remind ourselves our life could go on, even if it was painful. And it was the trip to start to learn that we could find a little laughter, happiness, and even possibly some joy again. No money could buy those things, but money sure helped us search for them.

If you come across someone you believe isn't handling a situation the way you might handle it, or you don't like how they are handling it, it is probably better you step away. Don't take the casserole, don't donate to the cause, and don't expect anyone in crisis to behave as you would behave in your non-crisis (or even in crisis!). Everyone is different and responds to situations differently. Offer the benefit of the doubt. For us, the magnitude of Sawyer being gone (*forever!*), the weight of our grief, and everything associated with it was too much to handle in and of itself. We did not need any judgmental criticism on top of it all. Do exercise a little grace and extend the assumption to others that most people who are grieving, especially during and after such a major personal loss, are handling things the best way they can to survive. It will serve everyone better than exercising or expressing judgment.

## The corollary to the above: Don't ask, "How are you?"

I know, it's hard. It is an instinct, an automated cultural response. I get it. But. I'm not well. Most people going through any type of trial are not well. I don't really want to talk about my most intimate trauma and the subsequent fallout in the grocery store soda aisle. Finn actually won a speech contest about this very notion at BYU in the semester after Sawyer died. I won't steal his ideas, but he talked a lot about how this phrase came to be and what some good alternatives are, such as "Good to see you today," "I've been thinking about you," or my favorite from the 1950s, "How hops it?," which was considered a general greeting in lieu of "Hello."

Because here's the other side of it too. Maybe, maybe we are having an okay day but that too comes loaded with emotion. Perhaps we have managed somehow to keep ourselves together for a day and actually feel like the clouds are starting to part and then with your three words, your "How's it going?," brings to mind all the ways things are terrible. This isn't to say truly asking someone how they are and how you can help isn't important, even necessary. It means we need to abolish the casual automaton blurting out of "How are you?" If you truly desire to know how I am doing in my trial, find ways to engage me in a private, personal way. Not in line at the post office.

## Just because you believe something is true doesn't mean you should share it.

When I was having a public meltdown at the Christmas parade two months after Sawyer's passing, my friend Gail told me about her first meltdown in public after her son died. She related an incident from the first Christmas following her son's tragic passing. She was in Walmart (nothing good happens in Walmart, I'm just saying . . .) and someone whom she didn't know well but who knew her and of her circumstances approached her. "I am so sorry for your loss. But you know, at least he is in a much better place!" She was shocked, angry, and in awe something so terrible would be said in such a public place. Embarrassed, she said, "I dropped the groceries I was carrying, stomped on the Christmas ornament I was about to purchase and cried, 'There is no better %$#@* place!,' and I turned and ran out of the store and cried uncontrollably in my car for two hours." I have had my own version of this and it hurts. It stings and literally takes my breath away. I want to ask, "Which of your loved ones shall we send to this better place?"

## Don't call the media unless you have your facts.

All your facts. Don't make assumptions based on gossip. Just don't. Do I really need to explain this one further?

# Chapter 10

## *The Tasks of Grief*

FOR A LONG TIME AFTERWARDS, I DIDN'T LIKE TO LEAVE THE HOUSE. I still sort of don't. Various family members juggled to arrange time out of their complicated lives to enable their extended stay so we as a family could hibernate. Some days we relied on them heavily, other days they did little. I think at times they wondered if they were helpful because there were a lot of moments where they were not "doing anything." To those who were present, your presence alone was important. It meant I knew that if I wanted to try a task, I could. Conversely, I knew if I couldn't pick up Sterling from preschool or sweep the floor after someone spilled a box of cereal, I didn't have to do it because someone else would.

I finally realized I was going to have to rebuild my life and a huge part of my life is shuttling people around. I decided I would muster the strength to take Sterling to preschool. It was the middle of November, a dark and depressing morning and not just because of my task. Some might question my use of the word "task." After your child dies (I had to write and rewrite that phrase five times just now, wanting to express it differently and realizing part of your pain is acknowledging there is no other way to say it), *everything* is a task. Breathing is a task. Eating is a task. Loving is a task. Living is a task. You get the point. On that day, my task involved getting out of bed, showering, putting on clothes that wouldn't end in me as an internet meme, driving Sterling to preschool, getting out of the car, talking to people, seeing people, and somehow surviving it all.

Preschool had its own wall of affiliated memories I had to break through. When I rushed to be near Sawyer's side, I left all other things behind, including Sterling and Grayson. Sterling was slated to get out of preschool soon after my arrival at the ER. I sent a panicked message to the preschool answering machine authorizing anyone who showed up from Jack's office to take her home and left it. The preschool swept into action. They found a makeshift lunch for Sterling and let her stay the extra hour and a half for the lunch and learn session she wasn't signed up to attend. The principal of the middle school who also had a child attending the preschool went and picked Sterling up with another person from Jack's office and got her nestled in at one of their homes. We even got an assuring text of her playing with dinosaurs with her new friend and laid that concern to rest. Like it or not, while we had a crisis to handle, we still had other children we needed to secure.

Back to the preschool, I knew it wasn't just another day of shuttling. I wore sunglasses in spite of the dreary overcast morning. I unbuckled Sterling and gathered all the courage I could muster, grabbed her hand and we started walking in. A woman from my book club who doesn't normally drop off her daughter was the first person I saw. She was leaving as I was approaching the building. By habit, as we approached, she asked, "Hey! How are you?," and I instantly bowed my head. She sort of shook her head and we subtly acknowledged the awkwardness and both kept going in our opposite directions. How was I ever supposed to emerge from my heartbreak? I knew I wasn't strong enough to deflect people for the rest of my life, and I also knew I couldn't just smile and proceed as though all was well. Nonetheless, sunglasses on, I made it into the school and back out to the car with little incident. I proceeded to sit in my car and cry because this seemingly little task had taken all my strength. Re-emerging into the world also reminded me that for us, life as we had known it was over but for the rest of the world, the earth kept spinning and life just kept moving.

Getting out and going places posed huge challenges but being at home was no cake walk either. Yes, I felt more comfortable at home secluded from seeing others and others seeing me, but it was also filled with memories of Sawyer. Memories are a tricky thing. My computer in sleep mode would scroll photos of the family, lots of them of Sawyer obviously. Every time I walked past the laptop, I would struggle to catch my breath. I loved seeing the pictures of him, but they also stopped my heart every time. I was telling my therapist this, and she said, "Why don't you change the sleep mode to generic pictures instead of your family outings?" How dare she? How dare she suggest I banish memories of my sweet boy? I felt like removing those would be a rejection of him and the beginning of our forgetting. I brushed off her suggestion until a few days later. Crying as I went to throw something in the trash, I realized we were still in first aid mode. We needed to do whatever needed to be done to continue breathing, to maneuver through the day without collapsing. And for me that meant removing the constantly flashing pictures of Sawyer from the computer. I cried as I set the default wallpaper to generic shots of worldwide geography, but I did it. A few days later, I noticed something. I hadn't cried every time I stepped into the kitchen to do some mundane task. The tears were still close to the surface and often came but for different reasons or other triggers, and they didn't catch me off guard as often as they did in the kitchen. One day I know I will change my computer settings back again, knowing those memories are there and will be critical for my survival. But for now, it was okay to just breathe at the sight of waterfalls.

There were the smaller tasks like computer settings to deal with at home but there were also the humongous tasks to be done. Grayson and Sawyer had shared a room. Sawyer shared our home and his fingerprints were literally everywhere! Our boy was a dirty boy! Cleaning and clearing out his stuff has been exhausting and we are nowhere near finished. I anticipate the process will take years. It's not just the physical labor piece of it, but the emotional tax is extremely high. I can't believe how much the expenditure of emotions drains me physically.

For a while we left his room untouched.

The first bout of cleaning happened almost immediately once we were home from the hospital because so many people were coming to the house. While we left his room alone, we needed help just getting bathrooms cleaned and the playroom straightened. I asked Finn if he thought he could handle the playroom and he said he could. I didn't ever want any of the children tasked with an assignment that would be too emotional for them, so we really tried to do a lot of asking and communicating, which was exhausting in its own right.

Finn came to me and said he had gotten the playroom into good working order quickly because it was already pretty clean for the most part. While Sawyer was in California, Grayson mostly hung out in their bedroom and in my room. So, cleaning the playroom was mostly messes from Grayson and Sawyer from . . . *before*. Finn asked if I wanted to see something funny or if I thought it would hurt too much. My personality is such that I always want something funny, even if it includes tears. Finn found several empty Doritos bags, hot chocolate cups, and dirty socks stuffed in various places around the playroom. Under the couch, behind pillows, in between board games, in the windowsill, at the bottom of the basket of blankets. The culprit was always Sawyer. It was his ten-year-old self. He couldn't, nay, wouldn't, put his trash in the trash can and always shed his socks wherever he took them off, which was everywhere! I cried as he showed the loot. I smiled too though. It was powerful because I knew in that moment the task of removing Sawyer's essence from our home would be painful and never ending. It's not that I wanted to "de-Sawyer-ify" the house. Quite the contrary. However, the unexpected jabs of seeing something reminding me of Sawyer everywhere I turned was like repeatedly getting stabbed in my heart.

Much of his stuff to this day sits around the house, friendly albeit sad reminders of his exuberance and magic. I anticipate for the next many years there will be grief tasks that need to be done, but I needed to start somewhere. My friend Jenn, who had been an acquaintance up until this trauma, had come over to help me go through bins in the attic. It wasn't to go through Sawyer's current wardrobe at the time, that still sits in the attic. It was a different yet necessary clearing. It was going through and purging all the clothes Sawyer would never have the chance to wear. Keeping our children in clothes without stains and holes was not a cheap endeavor. With three boys, I saved anything in good shape. There were several rubber bins filled with suits too big and sweaters not yet the right size for Sawyer. Yet. Now, never. I didn't think this task would be as hard as seeing a shirt he would regularly wear to basketball practice, another he'd wear to church every week, the sneakers he loved and didn't get the chance to wear out, or the winter hat his dad bought him in China. Those pieces were all deeply sorrowful to see. These clothes were different, nevertheless difficult to see. The acutely personal pain of knowing these bins were filled with clothes his brothers wore but he would not need was its own version or torture. Torture, I was finding, was not in short supply.

It wasn't just the clothes. I debated whether or not to share this story but in the name of opening ourselves in our grief and building empathy, I decided to go for it. It's perfectly Sawyer and it offers a revelation about our parenting: we weren't perfect. Now that we've covered that, we may proceed. Sawyer liked science, and if I hadn't known better, I'd have guessed his science fair project was about petrifying sandwiches. Throughout his entire 4$^{th}$ grade year, we would find Tupperware with old sandwiches in them all over the house. I can't tell you all the places we would find sandwiches. All kinds of sandwiches. Peanut butter, turkey, cheese, you name it, we found it. Often months and months too late. Somehow being in the Tupperware sealed in the stench, until it didn't, and then we would go on the hunt. He once ruined a backpack because he let the smell get so bad it was irreversible and after several launderings and sun-soakings the bag had to be tossed. You might ask, how can parents not notice all the missing Tupperware? We noticed. He was eight and nine years old. By evening he managed to lose shoes he had been wearing that day. We just figured the Tupperware offered another win for the lost and found bin somewhere. Either there or in a cafeteria trash can, never to be seen again. How could an involved parent not smell the stink? We didn't, until we did, as I said.

We tried every method we could think of to remedy the problem. We let him buy lunch some days, but he didn't like to buy it all the time. We bought different meats and cheeses he supposedly liked more than others for his sandwiches. We tried talking to him about why he wasn't eating the sandwiches, he couldn't say. We tried punishing him for the science experiments, he didn't quit. We tried withholding privileges, he would find something else to do, something different to eat. We were a communicative family, but for some reason he wouldn't offer any insight into why he was hiding the sandwiches, and more importantly, why he wasn't eating the sandwiches. One day the summer before he started the sixth grade, which turned out to be our last summer together, we had a long talk.

"Sawyer, you are going to be in middle school now. People who don't know your level of performance will be watching you and expecting more out of you, including us as your parents. You need to take responsibility for your work, responsibility for your behavior. Part of that is this lunch drama and the nasty sandwiches. Plus, I need your brain to work at full capacity and it can't do that if you don't get some good protein at lunch. Just tell me. Once and for all, what's the deal with the sandwiches?"

"I guess, Mom, I just really don't like sandwiches."

"That's it? You just don't like sandwiches? Why have you never said anything about it until now? We have given you plenty of opportunities to speak up."

"I don't know, I just didn't."

We had been finding those sandwiches everywhere for a year. Especially under his bed. And in his drawers. His entire fourth grade year was one disgusting find after the next. I don't know why it took us so long to crack the code, but after a year we finally got Sawyer to open up. He hated sandwiches. I've said it before, kids are strange. We spent the week before school started looking up sandwich alternatives on websites. We went to Costco and bulked up on said alternatives. We bought frozen burritos (ones only Sawyer liked, beef and green chili, so Grayson wouldn't steal them). We bought the supplies to make a month's worth of egg muffins, bagel pizzas, and other freezable items for Sawyer's lunches. We were organized and on top of it.

Fast forward to January of what would have been halfway through his sixth-grade year, about three months after he died. I decided it was time to clean out the freezer. People had been so generous with food. We live in the South. Strangers deal with death in different ways. Southerners don't know a stranger and deal with death by stuffing its face. Neighbors we had never met were bringing meal upon meal. One neighbor came by whom we had never met but who knew Sawyer. Turns out one winter he and Lucas had gone over to her house a few times to see if she needed help with her lawn or shoveling snow. She came by and introduced herself and expressed her condolences. She said, "I know we don't know each other, but I knew your boy. He was such a kind and sweet child. Even though we are strangers, I want you to know I have seen things in my life. I have seen some terrible things and I am strong. I am a strong woman. When everyone leaves, and you want to scream or talk to someone, don't scream at the walls. Don't talk to the walls, they can't listen. I am a good listener, and I will be here for you. Also, I brought a pizza. (Insert long pause.) It's *double* pepperoni." I was tearful at her wonderfully kind gesture of extending an arm of friendship to someone she hadn't known. And I was laughing. It was like she knew pepperoni pizza wasn't enough, we needed "double pepperoni" to get through this crisis. She was right.

So, while the pizza, double pepperoni, had been finished off quickly, there was a lot of other food left so it went to the freezer. We weren't able to get to it in those first few days and weeks so our caretakers put the food in our freezer knowing once they were gone, we would not have to cook for a while. I mention again my extreme gratitude for all the food. It would prove to sustain us long after the quiet settled and we were presented with rebuilding our lives anew and establishing a new routine. Before Sawyer passed away, I loved to cook. I usually started the meal during Sterling's nap time and had everything ready to put in the oven at the appropriate time so I wouldn't be bogged down with food prep after school. After school was the time I liked most to spend with the kids, hearing about their days, helping them with their homework, bailing on their homework so we could go to the park and play or ride bikes at the dead end of our street. Mealtime seemed overwhelming after Sawyer passed and all of our people had returned to their lives. I didn't want to cook. I didn't want to cook for four people. It was too few and taste buds too restrictive. Sawyer was my adventurous eater. The freezer meals people brought made it so I didn't have to endure the emotional torture I felt when I walked into the kitchen. But the freezer was bursting at the seams and I didn't know what was in it. The time had come to do an inventory of everything left so I could be sure to use it and not have anything go to waste.

Of course, that's when it happened. The foil pans and foreign Tupperware lined the freezer shelves, but so did the memories. The stacks of sandwich substitutes we'd made together the summer prior, gobs of eggs on English muffins and bagel pizzas, and the green chili bean burritos we'd bought just for Sawyer jumped out at me and punched me in the face. Sawyer was everywhere. It was powerful to have his presence everywhere, but it was also painful, almost damaging. It feels wrong to even say those words, but it was true. The tasks that were hard independent of the memories were proving to be exponentially more difficult than I assumed they'd be. I expected his footprint to be found in a lot of places. His room, the yard, in the laundry, on the walls, shoes by the door. There were times it was too much, though, and I needed an escape. I needed a safe place to go in my distractions and not be consumed with all the feelings I couldn't juggle. The freezer. It should've been my distraction for the day, not my trigger. It was that day I realized there was no escape. There was no safe space. Even the places and tasks once mundane and benign were now triggers to the gut-wrenching loss Sawyer's death had gifted me. There was no way around the tasks, I had to move through each and every one of them.

People would make comments about how hard the firsts were going to be for our family. The first Christmas without him, the first birthday of his and all of ours without him, the first day of school he isn't there for, our first Easter egg hunt without him. All of that was true. What we weren't prepared for were all the little tasks that were firsts we had to endure. Obviously, the big ones were when people stepped in and offered help and consoling. There was no way everyone could offer help for all the little tasks that brought with them big emotions. What people could do is recognize it wasn't just the big firsts that were tough. Every single day brought something difficult to handle or too overwhelming to consider which made all of the things people said to us, expected of us, required of us and even demanded of us compound our grief.

It is another reason why I want to share our story. I want people to understand there are so many grief moments in every day and when someone is experiencing such a loss, we need to be overly compassionate, overly understanding, and avoid expecting people to function in the same way you might have expected them to before their loss. They are forever changed and handling those changes take time. A lot of time. Great if you can lighten their load by sharing in the tasks. If you can't, you can always offer a little grace and give someone an extra pass now and then. Grieving is an all-consuming full-time job, and none of us have the option to have time stand still while we grieve, heal, pull ourselves together and find some semblance of ourselves again. The job is infinitely bigger than what you might expect and isn't complete after the first year is over, or the second, or so on. We have to go to work, raise children, foster relationships, and keep our life afloat even as we carry the weight of grief. That said, any help in the big and little tasks of grieving you can offer, not just in the immediate aftermath, but in the years to come, will always be appreciated as a way to mourn with those who mourn. If the help you can offer is in the form of a listening ear, extra patience, or repeated cheerleading, continue offering. When you have friends, colleagues, coworkers, or anyone with whom you share a relationship, you can foster that relationship by attending to them in their grief, and long after you think their grief should be over. I believe it is one of our duties as a friend, and really as part of our humanity.

# Chapter 11

# *The Quest to Find My People*

My dear friend Ann is a psychologist. One of her areas of expertise is abnormal/deviant sexual behaviors, so she really was no help to me as a psychologist, but she did say something once that impacted me. I needed to escape the weight of my life, but things were falling apart around me. Living three hours apart, Ann suggested we meet halfway for an evening together. It's important to say that I didn't call her and tell her, "Things are falling apart, I need to escape, help me." She was one of the people who routinely called, texted, or even texted to see if it was all right if she called. It was in those conversations and texts she sensed I needed a break. If she had adhered to the "Call me if you need anything" philosophy, which many people did, this much needed break would've never happened. Nonetheless, we had less than a few hours together, but it served me well. She listened. I talked. I cried and talked some more. I spoke freely and didn't worry about her judging what I said. There are so many confusing and mixed feelings surrounding child loss, judgment about anything from anyone was the last thing I needed.

I had been visiting some online groups and gone to a couple of in-person grief groups for parents who had lost children. Personally, in my journey, I had found them to be unhelpful. I know they can be a great source of comfort to some people. But not for me. Particularly the one I had gone to in person. I felt like I caught a glimpse of my life twenty years down the road and it scared me. It seemed like every-thing was manifested in extremes with both the online and in-person groups. People were in one of two camps. My use of hyperbole is not to offend but to magnify the two extremes I felt I was being pushed towards. There were the "My deceased child and I are good now, I have found peace! I celebrate her angel wings! Life is awesome and we have faith, so we are fine and yay—let's run a marathon!" par-ents. They are in the rainbows and unicorns camp. Then there was the other group, the one I fear. Everyone in this camp only shared stories of demise and despair. Even ten, twenty, thirty years beyond their tragedies this group was still almost drowning in their pain. I could not find a middle ground amongst the grievers I encountered. As Ann and I spoke over mediocre milkshakes, she said, "The people you are seeking aren't going to these groups. They aren't so sorrowful every day that they seek comfort from these meetings. But they aren't so strong or comfortable enough that they go out in the world as the model of healing for all to see, either. They quietly go about their business, sad some days and happy others, and have found a way to incorporate their grief into their lives in a healthy way. You need to find those people." She was right, and so began my quest to find those people who would become my people.

But first, a caveat. Grieving sucks. Burying your child is an immeasurable tragedy and filled with a sorrow deeper and more intense than anything even moderately comparable. In whatever way people need to cope and at whatever pace, I respect their journey. I needed mentors for my journey and the two extremes just didn't mesh with my life and what I needed. So, it's not a knock on either camp, it's an acknowledgement that I personally needed something else. Just because I couldn't find what I needed in those groups doesn't dimin-ish their value. I know many who can and do find solace there and I'm grateful they exist. Grieving the loss of your child is something no one should ever have to do alone or in silence. And how you choose to travel the path is never something anyone should judge.

But back to my quest. Enter: The Klines.

I met Paul Kline fairly soon after arriving in Amelia because he was one of Sawyer's Cub Scout leaders. His son Caleb had been a friend of Sawyers. I will never forget the time he told me about their child loss. We were doing a bike road rally for Cub Scouts and the kids were cycling the Veteran's Building repeatedly and I was wasting time until it was over. I had tried to walk laps beside the riders to get my steps in but quickly realized these bikers had no recognition of walkers and I'd need to find something else to do or risk a crash. I loitered, as not many people in the tight-knit community were interested in small talk with a relative stranger. But Paul was kind. I struck up a conversation with him and told him I thought his son was a good friend to Sawyer and expressed my gratitude. I asked him if he had other children. (By the way, I never do this anymore. What has always seemed like a benign question to me has since become a loaded one, so who's to say it isn't loaded for other people. I am embarrassed for my ignorance.) With a smile on his face, he said Caleb had an older brother Josh who was in middle school and another brother between Caleb and Josh who had died. I said I was sorry, befuddled as I said it, I am sure. Paul said, "Thank you. It explains the big gap between Caleb and Josh." I got the sense he felt he had to explain, but I don't know for sure. I totally get it now, as Grayson and Sterling are nine years apart. To outsiders I am sure it seems like there is a story. And oh, what a story! Anyway, in the moment Paul told me about his son passing, I had so many thoughts run through my mind.

I had seen Paul and his wife Gail at different events and she seemed like someone I could have been friends with but hadn't had the occasion to meet up with socially. I do that: scan people who could be my friends. It's odd but I have always done it. I was a young mom when I had Finn, I was an old mom when Sterling came into our family, the middle felt like a wash. Finding people with children of a similar age, who were in a similar life circumstance, proved difficult in our new town. Having moved from my network of friends to a new place where my husband was a boss for half of the county meant diminishing returns on the friend quest. Yet Gail had stood out to me. She was quiet. When we spoke, she was funny. But there was something quiet and reserved about her. In the middle of the bike rally as Paul was speaking, all I could think about was Gail. I want Jack to write a book about grieving as a dad, because I think he has a story all his own, but I am embarrassed that as I was standing in front of this grieving father, all I could think of was Gail.

Gail had a son in Sawyer's class, turned out her older son was in Grayson's French class, and now we shared the uncommon experience of losing a son. Other than briefly chatting with her spouse and exchanging emails about classroom party supplies during various holidays, I had known she had lost a son, but nothing more. Driving home from the hospital after Sawyer died, I thought about the exchange Paul and I had at the bike rally. It came to me clearly and I obsessed over it. Was I compassionate enough when he told me about his son? Did I blow him off because it was an awkward conversation? Was it even awkward? How did I resume the conversation? Did I? I just remember him handling the conversation so well. I couldn't stop thinking about how I would convey the greatest loss of my life in one sentence and with such dignity. Sawyer was our bridge. Grayson and Sterling were bridged by Sawyer in so many ways. How would I ever convey this to strangers in the supermarket who ask how many children we have? And harder still, how would we ever cross the divide between the two of them? It's a challenge with his loss so fresh, I hadn't had time to consider, but would plague me even still. But because Paul had shared this knowledge with me, I knew my quest to find a friend would start with Gail. Paul obviously didn't know this would come when he shared the information. But it taught me that grief and sadness, whatever the cause, isn't something we have to hide or brush over. You never know when what you share will have a profound impact on someone else.

Even while we were still in the hospital lying in the bed with Sawyer waiting for the transplant team, I had a lot of time to think, and at one point thought of Gail. I thought, "Now I guess we have to be friends because I need a friend who has lived this earth-shattering grief to get me through this . . ." But friendships don't just work that way. You can't just decide who you want to be your friend and voilà! Suddenly they are at your door to pick you up for a day of shopping and comfort. But that is sort of what happened with Gail and I, minus the shopping.

At the conclusion of Sawyer's Celebration of Life, Gail approached me. Having exchanged a few business-oriented emails about classroom parties, we were not close friends, but she embraced me. I really have had no choice but to become a hugger after all of this *life* has happened, so I hugged her back. She said she'd been wanting to reach out to me since she heard the news but wasn't sure where or when or how. She said she'd been praying for me, for our family, and she would be in touch. And she was. Someone who had her own story and her own pain reached out to me and over the course of the next several months, she and Paul comforted Jack and I with long emails, cry-fests, and most of all an understanding and listening ear, an ear with no judgment and complete compassion.

My first truly public outing after Sawyer died with no one to shield me from the onslaught of people was the local Christmas parade. Grayson didn't want to go. No surprise. Sterling was four. How was I supposed to keep denying her childhood delights because I couldn't manage my grief? I couldn't. I carry so much guilt about not being the perfect parent for Sawyer, I knew I had to muster the best version of myself for that day, and it involved going to the Christmas parade. My understanding friend, Angel, had reached out to me and offered a space of solace to watch the parade. She said her office was going to be open on the parade route, they were going to have food for friends to enjoy and she wouldn't mind looking after Sterling if my emotions got the better of me and I needed to retreat for a breath. I thanked her for her offer and made no commitment. But as the clock ticked closer to 4 p.m., I got myself dressed and had my mom drop Sterling and me off at the parade. Jack was teaching his university class, so I was going it alone.

I walked into the space, saw Angel and a host of people I didn't know, and started to cry. I find my emotions these days are unpredictable. Everyone kept saying, "If you are depressed, you can get on medication." I can't tell you how many people told me a version of this sentiment. I appreciated their intentions of trying to de-stigmatize depression, but I wasn't depressed. I was grieving. Regardless, I was tearing up and Angel's daughter and husband whisked Sterling away to grab a plate full of goodies and Angel just let me cry. I won't pretend to know where all the tears came from, other than the obvious. I watched the parade with Sterling briefly from in and out of the office, but since she was enjoying the company of a teenage girl attending to her every need, I mostly sat in the back of the room. Gail came in, she'd heard I was in Angel's office. News travels quickly in small towns, and she'd wanted to comfort me.

We hadn't really had a lot of time to chat at Sawyer's celebration for obvious reasons and while we had exchanged a few emails about my new life and getting us all together, we hadn't had time to talk. There, amidst the shrimp cocktail and cheery well-wishers coming in and out watching the Christmas parade, we shared the intimate details of our lives. We don't hang out all the time, we haven't become best friends, but I know she is there. Her gentle presence is a shadow I can turn to when I need it. Without her willingness to let me see her pain and sadness, I truly believe it would have taken me so much longer to be willing to share my own. Jack and I have developed a friendship with Gail and Paul that Jack and I will forever cherish.

Another listening ear came as a card arrived at our door a couple of months after Sawyer died. People use the phrase "Child loss is a club no one asked to join." I hate that phrase. I'm not entirely sure why, I guess because it has so many implications. It implies there are enough of us to be considered our own group, which is entirely too true, and still horribly sad. It also recalls my associations with clubs—groups of people who gather together to find unity in a common goal or purpose, but usually light-hearted or fun. This "club" entails neither of those aspects, but it does bring an unexpected and powerful unity.

You remember the little boy Isaac from Amelia, who died just prior to Sawyer? His mother was the one who had sent us the card. She included in it her name, Nicole, her phone number, and a suggestion that perhaps we should get together to talk now that we shared a similar life tragedy. We didn't know each other previously and we had little in common. As the superintendent, Jack had gone to represent the schools and convey his condolences at the time of Isaac's passing, but that was the extent of our connection. Strange how life works sometimes, isn't it? At the time, literally just weeks before Sawyer died, Jack was struck to his core by Isaac's passing. He talked to me a couple of times about the injustice of it, how tragic it was and how helpless he felt towards this family whom he didn't know but for whom he wanted to reach out. He just wasn't sure what to do or how to help. They had no other children in the district so he couldn't link himself to the family and help in that way, and so time passed and we shed many tears for them, and we let it be.

I think about that a lot. I remember that after Isaac had passed, I had seen an article in the local paper showing the teachers and students all wearing orange because it was one of Isaac's favorite colors. I thought as I read the paper, "How terribly sad for this mother," and I went about my day. I did it, you've done it. We have all done it. Something terrible happens and it strikes a nerve with us and makes us feel uneasy, uncomfortable, and reminds us of our own fate. It makes us hug our loved ones a little tighter and then we put it out of our mind because it is painful and we don't want to feel that pain. It goes against teachings central to our very nature, our basic instinct to find and dwell in happiness. Thinking about children dying, especially unexpectedly, tragically, and for no reason at all is the antithesis of happiness so I put it and this family out of my mind.

What I forgot, what I think we often all forget, is that we also know is that we live in communities and villages. We are counseled to mourn with those who mourn and comfort those who stand in need of comfort. We can't do that if we live our lives as though we are an island unto ourselves. I am embarrassed and have apologized to Isaac's mom because had it not been for Sawyer's death, I probably would have never met her or been able to share her loss with her or offer a hand to lift her in her healing. I didn't know her, and I am not really the type of person to go out of my way to speak with the lady in line in front of me at the grocery store about the weather, never mind reaching out to a total stranger and try to understand her loss and her grief. We've been over this about me. And this wasn't just any grief. It was big, the biggest! Burying your child is impossible and I don't think I ever would have had the nerve or courage to be of comfort to her. I was entirely wrong to not reach out more. Now, I am not suggesting every time you read about the tragedy of a stranger to call them out of the blue and descend on them like a vulture in the name of offering comfort. I'm not suggesting every time you hear of something sad happening you should send flowers or drive over and deliver ice cream. But I am suggesting we could all do a little more, extend ourselves a little more, and open ourselves up a little more to those grieving, for whatever the reason. Both of these women, Gail and Nicole, I connected with because we are living a similar life tragedy.

We all have experienced knowing someone with some sort of grief. In the months following Sawyer's death, Jack reconnected with two friends from college who separately were going through tough divorces. Jack had many long and late-night conversations with both of his friends where they talked a lot about the things they had lost and were losing. One night one of them said, "I feel badly talking to you about this. My divorce is terrible, but it is nothing compared to the pain and suffering you must be going through." After they hung up the phone, Jack approached me and told me what his friend had said. Jack responded, "The strange thing is, as soon as he said that, I bristled. Not because I was offended but because I didn't quite believe it. Yes, Sawyer dying has broken us into pieces and we will never be the same. But the pieces can be picked up and mended in eternity. He is losing his eternal family and that is a pain and sorrow that must be worse. Or at least as bad." I am not saying either of them is right or wrong. What I am saying is that on some level sorrow is sorrow. There are different levels, causes of, and experiences with grief. I would never qualify or quantify grief from one event over another event or one circumstance with another. But what I am saying is there are commonalities in grief. If we never share our grief, we cannot build our understanding of and empathy for grief. We can all serve as another person's grief companion and help someone else in their quest to find their people.

Even though Nicole and Gail and I share the trauma and tragedy of sudden child loss, I don't think that has to be the requirement for connection. Robyn from preschool and I connected over the loss of her home. Yes, Nicole and Gail were able to relate to me in an intimate way over the death of our children, but for all of these people, the connection resulted because they reached out. Nicole and Gail took something so private and so tragic and used it to connect with me. They sought me out, in spite of the fact that for both of them, it was out of their comfort zone. Do it! Get out of your comfort zone and lend an ear, offer a tissue, complicate your schedule to make time for those who could use your wisdom and life experience.

I have dear friends who I have known for years who are no less dear, but with whom I have lost my connection because they haven't reached out. Some promised they would come for a visit or even just call, but calendar dates were never actually offered and their number never showed up on my call list. I often wonder if the reality of my horror was too close for them, they knew Sawyer too well, and they knew that if it could happen to me then it could happen to them. It almost felt like they perceived tragedy to be contagious. Tragedy is not contagious. Perhaps grief is a little contagious, but I needed old friends to be willing to put the mask on and enter the room. I don't think I will ever know or understand why some reached out and some abandoned me in my hour of need. That is not my quest. I try not to hold too much judgment because I have some of my own I am working to abandon. For me, seeing people with ten-year-old children is quite difficult, so at Nicole's suggestion, I try to just appreciate old friendships for where they got me and focus on the friendships who are taking me the rest of the way.

Conversely, I have other friends who, in my time of need, have stepped up and offered a deeper friendship to me when I needed it most. I didn't have to ask them or tell how I needed their friendship. They just reached out, persistently. They called. They texted. They sent cards and prayers. They offered love and persistent attention. They paid bills for us that were threatening to crush us. They offered compassion in so many ways. They will forever be the angels I know God placed in my life because of how they have reached out, even though many of them don't believe in God or angels. For Jack, the connection was made with his friends, some who he's known forever and some who he's met in the wake of our tragedy, but all were individuals who reached out. They knew he was in crisis and they didn't wait for their lives to be in order to check in with him. All of our people made the first move not knowing how their actions would be perceived. And it has made all the difference in our healing journey.

# Chapter 12

## *The Battle for My Faith*

A COUPLE OF MONTHS AFTER SAWYER DIED, I WAS ON FACEBOOK AND a friend from high school reached out to me privately. We weren't close, but that's the thing about grief. It draws in other grievers. I have to think it's in part because so few people seem to understand grief so when we are grieving, others who have grieved seek to offer comfort known by one who has experienced grief. My friend had watched her very faithful parents die slow, painful, and complicated deaths. She heard their prayers for their suffering to be relieved and it didn't come in time. She watched them die over a long period of time and the journey she witnessed wasn't pretty. In the end, it was a journey she felt robbed them of their dignity and her of her deep and abiding faith in God. As we messaged back and forth about the pain of loss, she said, "Well, I hope in the end you don't lose your faith because watching my parents die cost me mine." I am so grateful for her sharing such an intimate part of her life with me. It is something I needed to hear. It is counsel I have held to tightly as I have grieved Sawyer leaving this world too soon. It has been hard work to keep my faith and something I actively attend to every single day.

The gospel of Jesus Christ anchors us, it gives us hope for the eternities and provides a foundational knowledge about the afterlife and joy we will feel being reunited with our loved ones. Faith anchors us but what are the tools we need here and now to get through to that point, to make it to the next step, to endure to the end? For those who experience grief at any level, what do we do with our mortal selves until then? For me it is likely another forty years on earth, for others even longer. What do we do, how do we cope? Those are all questions with no concrete answers, but they are questions I have heard many faithful grievers ask.

Somehow, somewhere along the way, many in the believing world have decided that being faithful and being sorrowful are mutually exclusive. It's as though there is a feeling that if you have "enough" faith, you won't be sad, won't mourn, or won't grieve. At least not for very long because, after all, [insert all clichés about heaven and being with God and God's plan]. Some of you are reading that sentence and thinking, "Oh, she called them clichés so that must mean she doesn't believe the doctrines about heaven and God." That is entirely untrue. But I have a message for the world about faith and grieving. And quite frankly, so does God in the scriptures, but we will get there.

Returning to church was difficult and remains so to this day, which is hard because I have been a churchgoer almost my entire life. I have found joy in service and a peace that surpasses all understanding as I participate fully in my church responsibilities both on a personal level and on a leadership level. I worked hard for my testimony as a young adult and it is something I treasure above all else, so add the comfort and joy of church attendance to the list of things we lost when Sawyer died. I anticipate there will be a time down the road when it will bring more joy than pain and if it takes a very long time, so be it. Talk about triggers though! Try sitting in church where the first note of the opening hymn talks about death and dying and the last prayer of the last meeting talks about blessing everyone with safety and comfort. It is painful. It took us several weeks to go back to church even for just sacrament meeting. I remember well the first time Jack tried to go back. I knew I wasn't ready so I wasn't even trying to go and take the kids, but Jack wanted to at least partake of the sacrament. He got up that morning, showered, and got dressed, and almost made it out the door. The weight was too much, and the tears and the pain got the better of him and he crawled back into bed with me knowing we would try again another week. When we did make it back to church it wasn't to our specific congregation.

Geographically we are located on the outskirts of two buildings and thus two different congregations. One is twenty-five minutes south and one thirty minutes north. Our leader, President Lewis, was amazing during our time in the hospital and in the immediate aftermath. Once we got home, he made sure we had meals come in, he came to visit us regularly to listen, check on us, and check in on the children. In one of the visits, I told him I wasn't sure how I was ever supposed to go back to the building we had attended church in because Sawyer and his presence filled that space for me. The mere thought of returning crushed my soul.

I think there were a couple of reasons why it seemed so difficult. To understand where I was coming from you need to understand two things. First, the congregation was small. About 60 in attendance to sacrament meeting on a good day which meant about 10 children were in primary on a full day. I was in the primary leadership and worked closely with the children, namely Sawyer, each week. It was something I loved doing and loved being able to discuss the gospel and teach Sawyer exactly what he needed to learn. It is a time in my life I will always cherish, those small intimate discussions in that tiny primary room. Compounding my uneasy feelings was my experience with him the last Sunday I saw him alive. Remember, he had been in California the week prior to his death so I hadn't seen him in over a week. The Sunday before he left, he and I were literally the only ones in Primary. Sawyer and I alone for the lesson. At first, I shrugged off the idea of teaching, reasoning, "He hears this stuff from me all the time, we are just going to hang out and play a game or something." But then I thought again because the lesson was on prayer, something we had been talking about with Sawyer recently.

I decided we would proceed with the lesson. By then the pianist had come in and done music time with him. Since it was just the two of them, she gave him a private piano lesson where they worked on playing our family song, "Give, Said the Little Stream," so he could play it for us during Family Home Evening. Regrettably, we were never able to hear his version.

As I write that line, I struggle to catch my breath even still. There are so many nevers that weigh so heavily on me. We sat down and started talking about prayer and I told him a story from the church lesson plans about a church leader, Elaine S. Dalton. She had related a story about when her dad passed away. She was a youth and she and her mother prayed and prayed that her father, who had been rushed to the hospital unexpectedly, would be healed. He was not healed at that time and passed away a couple of days later. Elaine S. Dalton explained that her dad dying right then, after she pleaded with the Lord using all her might and faith, was a blow to her. She obviously wanted him to live and didn't understand why her prayers were not answered. I kid you not this was the story from that lesson, ask our pianist who was there. It was clearly a lesson for me, not Sawyer. The lesson continued that years later as an adult, she was sitting in General Conference (a time when, twice a year, members of The Church of Jesus Christ of Latter-day Saints listen to leaders speak about doctrine) listening to a speaker and her prayers about her dad were answered. He was not healed, but in a moment decades later, she had a powerful witness of what happened and knew her father was with God and her prayer was answered. Not when she wanted it answered, and not in the way she wanted it answered, but her answers came. Somehow, I was supposed to return to that little room with those final exchanges between Sawyer and I lingering in the walls and casting a shadow over my own prayers? I couldn't.

I was already struggling with my own prayers since Sawyer died. Did I continue to pray for Sawyer? If so, for what was I asking? Never mind the elephant in the room in regards to prayer. We had prayed in the hospital with all of our might. Many people prayed across the country and put Sawyer's name on prayer rolls in the temple. People more worthy and more faithful than me prayed for Sawyer. Prayer after prayer was offered in Sawyer's behalf, even prayers offering our own lives in exchange for his. Intimate, desperate, pleading prayers were offered for Sawyer to live. Sawyer died.

I struggled with prayer and what I should actually be asking for in my prayers. We are told to pray over our crops and fields, for our enemies, for the mundane and tangible, for things we have control over and things we have no control over. Why? For a long time I couldn't reconcile what I should be asking for in my prayers because clearly my big ask was denied so why bother with the little things? I finally came to a resolution, and, for me and for now, it works. Maybe you can get something out of it too. Prayer should be more about building a relationship with God, not trying to get answers or have God grant your requests, using God as your personal genie. I think about my earthly relationships. How do I build a relationship, whether it be with my spouse who I interact with daily or with a friend who lives across the country who I only see once a year? For any relationship I have to engage with that person. I have to open myself up and share my thoughts and feelings and tell them all the big things and little things that occur in my life. I tell them I don't want the rain to come because it will ruin my party, but if the rain comes, I don't blame them. I ask them to help me move the party inside. I've decided for me, that is what prayer is about, building an intimate relationship with God. Asking to communicate and open the dialogue between us, not asking, crossing my fingers and toes, I get what I ask for from Him.

As I have read and read and read more counsel from my church leaders and religious leaders of many faiths, I stumbled across this idea. When Christ was in the Garden of Gethsemane, He prayed for God to take away His suffering when He cried, "O My Father, if it be possible, let this cup pass from me: nevertheless not as I will, but as thou wilt" (Matt. 26:39). Christ continued in pain, bleeding from every pore as He took upon the sins of the world. Did God the Father not answer His prayer? He continued in pain and asked again, for the pain to be removed, knowing that was not how He would achieve the will of the Father. His prayer ("Thy will be done") was answered but His request (to remove the pain and sorrow) was denied. After Christ had taken upon Himself all of my sins, all of yours, all of everyone's, He surrendered His spirit. The idea is that there are times in our lives when, because we do not know the end game, we will ask for things and God will not give us what we request but He will indeed hear our prayer. Even when the answer we want doesn't come or look the way we think it should. We can still use our prayers to build a relationship with God, even if it is a tenuous relationship at times.

I can remember standing in the bathroom at the hospital staring into the mirror in the hall bathroom, deeply staring, searching. When Sawyer would go for a test and leave his room, I, too, would try and step out and take a lap and see some of the cheerleaders we had in the lobby. I would go into the bathroom just to be in a private space and sob. I would stare into that dirty, cracked mirror intensely. It was as though I thought if I would stare hard enough, God Himself would look back at me. I told him, "I know you can perform miracles. I have read about them. I have seen them in the lives of others. Show me a miracle. I believe. Sawyer should live despite the odds. Give me my miracle." And knowing, as the words were coming out of my mouth, knowing that was not the way things were going to go down, but I still had to say the words.

I absolutely cringe when I hear people talk about when they were "saved" (physically) because they prayed hard enough, paid their tithing on time, did a good deed for someone else, or were just generally being good, so their miracle came. That is not the doctrine. Miracles, whether of healing or otherwise, do not come simply because someone was worthy enough. We do not know why some prayers are answered one way and some another. That is faith. Faith is being all of those righteous things, doing all of those righteous things, *not* having your prayers answered immediately, not getting those miracles, and still not denying you know God.

When we were in the first several weeks after Sawyer's death, I was reading everything I could find from General Authorities on how to cope, how to grieve, how to breathe in the midst of tragedy. One of the talks I re-read over and over again was the talk by Elder Uchtdorf, "Fourth Floor, Last Door." This quote hit me in a profound way: ". . . there are more ways to see than with our eyes, more ways to feel than with our hands, more ways to hear than with our ears.". I even posted it on social media, I think more in an attempt to convince myself. My sweet love is no longer here for me to see with my eyes, touch with my hands, smell with my nose, kiss with my lips. I will not feel his bony hands in mine again. I will not patch up his skateboard scratches. I will not smell his stinky ten-year-old boy breath or post-basketball B.O. But reading these words, I needed to believe them, I wanted to believe them, and I need this promise from Elder Uchtdorf to be true. I still do. Elder Uchtdorf continues to quote the Little Prince, who says, "One sees clearly only with the heart. Anything essential is invisible to the eyes." As I struggle still through the tears, I have to know that I can still feel Sawyer in other ways. The same holds true for God. We cannot literally call Him when we need someone on the other line to hear a voice. We cannot ask for Him to physically carry our load when our packs are too heavy. We cannot reach out for a hug from Him when we are desperate and lonely. We must find other ways to connect with God.

My friend Sharon lost her son over fifteen years ago when he was in a car accident at age nineteen. She has been a guide for me through my grieving. I told her I believed what Elder Uchtdorf teaches, but I was struggling because I couldn't feel Sawyer the way I needed to feel him and at the frequency I wanted to connect with him. She offered this, "Maybe he is giving you space to heal. You are too raw, too sorrowful, and as his spirit comes near, you sense him. You feel him and you are overcome with emotions you are too fragile to handle right now. I believe that was true for me. Once more time had passed and I had settled into my sorrow a little more, his spirit could come reside with me and I could feel his presence and not get so unsettled and sad feeling him near me. Maybe the same will hold true for you." It made sense to me. Sawyer himself was a trigger for me. I believe he is watching, cheering, protecting, working, and hopefully playing, while he waits for me to be ready to connect with him in new ways. As I have thought about this possibility, I have thought about my relationship with God too. How much of our relationship do I blame on God not coming through for me or not connecting with me when really it is me unwilling or unable to connect with Him and it is I who needs to change myself to let His Spirit reside with me?

With Sawyer, we try to avoid making lists of all the things we cannot ever do with him again or even get to do with him at all. Instead, we try to focus on what we did do together and what we can do with him now, eventually, and in his name. We can remember him, tell stories about him, laugh and cry because of him, honor him by telling his story to others, acknowledge his Seven Gifts and encourage others to give the gift of life, and we can help each other as a family to never, ever forget him. The same holds true for God. Faith is similar, focusing on what we believe and what we can do with God and in His name right here and now, in the place we are at, instead of fretting over all the things we cannot do or see or explain about God. Elder Uchtdorf also says, "Faith is a strong conviction about something we believe—a conviction so strong that it moves us to do things that we otherwise might not do." We are taught faith is hoping for things we cannot see, but are true.

Faith is powerful. Faith can do many things, but faith cannot force our will upon God. No matter how much we try, not matter how worthy we are, no matter how much we want it, no matter how righteous our will may be.

I've mentioned I have been a voracious reader since Sawyer's death as I try to understand the world as it is now for me in my grief. I read anything and everything on grieving, on hope, on loss, on coping, on joy, on happiness, on healing versus curing, on the plan of salvation, on all of it. A friend shared an article with me. I believe it has profound doctrine in it. It is powerful in the way we approach sorrow and grief because of the terrible things we experience as part of being human here on earth. The general notion is better expressed by Christine Suhan:

> God's will is not an event that happens to us, it's how we respond to what happens. . . . There's hardly ever a justifiable reason for the bad things that happen in life. Tragic loss is not laced with inherent specs of good. I used to get so mad when people would say, "You can find good in every situation." That's just not true. There was nothing good about being raped. There is no good in murder or abuse. We have to create the good. We have to choose to respond in a way that brings good into an impossible situation. We have to choose to give purpose and meaning to our suffering.
>
> Not everything happens for a reason. But in everything that happens, there can be a reason to bring hope and healing to others. God can use our pain for a greater good if we choose to let Him in.

In the "Fourth Floor, Last Door," Dieter F. Uchtdorf also says,

> Faith means that we trust not only in God's wisdom but that we trust also in His love. It means trusting that God loves us perfectly, that everything He does—every blessing He gives and every blessing He, for a time, withholds—is for our eternal happiness. With this kind of faith, though we may not understand why certain things happen or why certain prayers go unanswered,

*we can know that in the end everything will make sense. . . . All will be made right. All will be well.*

In the end. It gives the concept of enduring to the end more weight, but possibly more joy—in the end.

Something we heard over and over again in the immediate aftermath, and still hear occasionally to this day is, "God has a Plan." Over and over. Waiting in the family room in the PICU, my dear friend kept saying this over and over again. I finally told her I loved her, I believed her, but if she said it again, I was going to ask security to take her out. Losing my sweet, magical Sawyer did not make sense. It is not good. There is nothing good about it, for me and my family anyway. My friend kept saying, "But God has a plan. Trust His plan." While removed from this situation, I understand this doctrine to be true, hearing these words in the moment did nothing to help me. It only made me want to hate God, because if taking Sawyer from me so abruptly was His plan, I hate His plan and by default Him for having such a terrible plan. I needed God on my side at that time more than ever, and I didn't need anything that would distance Him from me.

Accepting His plan was out of the question. I do not accept this version of the plan for my life to date. I acknowledge it, but on some days even that feels impossible. I do know that how I respond to our tragic and overwhelming loss is impactful. In my heart of hearts, I also want to believe the way I respond also has the potential to bring a measure of goodness to my life and to my family. While I feel the importance of including God in our healing journey, I am just trying to navigate how that looks. Grief has morphed many of my earthly relationships. Who am I to think it would not also impact heavenly relationships as well? I also believe Christ is always looking at what is best for us and can see our end game, eternal life with Him and our family. He has the gift, and I imagine the curse sometimes, of seeing the big picture. There are times when, in order to achieve that goal, our immediate requests might be denied, but our prayers will be answered. Accepting that I also believe in the notion that not everything happens for a reason, sometimes things just happen. We can't use God as our personal genie, asking Him to grant us certain things because we promise to engage in some things or avoid other things.

The Plan is more about how we turn to God to deal with what happens, not about the minutiae of what actually happens. I focus on the second half of the prayer more so than the first, the gratitude for what I have been given as opposed to the request for what I think I need. This has a direct impact on what I pray for and has impacted my prayers profoundly since Sawyer died. I offer a measure of gratitude for each tender mercy surrounding Sawyer's death. I offer thanks for the blessings in my life, even if some days it is just the ability to shower or the pizza delivery service. I also pray more for the intangibles that build me as a person and grow me closer to God and for strength to endure whatever happens each day. I pray for understanding, not to know all things, but to understand I cannot know all things, and the hope that I can find peace in that uncertainty. I focus my prayers on the "but if not, help me learn <insert characteristic> to deal with what does happen."

Continuing my conversation with President Lewis about returning to church after Sawyer died was depressing. Church before Sawyer died had been a little challenging since we had left Radford. The small building we attended church in was difficult to attend when we first moved into the area. A large portion of the branch was related to each other. Before I was in the Primary, the leadership consisted of many of the children's aunts and cousins. The chatter before and after church often revolved around family reunions or birthday parties or activities our family, specifically our children, were not included in, and it was hard on all of us. Weeks had passed when we first arrived, and we didn't get any callings. Between Jack being a bishop and high counselor prior to moving here, and me always in some auxiliary presidency, we felt unneeded and unwanted. Much of our feelings were of our own making, nonetheless, it was a time when we as a family drew closer. We unified ourselves and gave ourselves tasks on Sunday to feel more connected to our Savior and to grow our testimonies. It was a time our family was close, maybe closer than at any other time, in regard to our collective Sunday worship and general church participation. And now? Now I was supposed to go back to that space, back to the place where I shared so deeply with Sawyer and he was not going with me? Impacted, too, by Finn being away at college as well? I knew I could not go back to that building any time soon and I knew that if

I didn't go to church at all I would indeed lose my faith, as my friend had cautioned me about.

We spoke with President Lewis about our concerns and fears and he took them to the loving stake presidency. The members of the stake presidency had been by our side at different times during Sawyer's hospital stay and had given us blessings and said prayers with us. I know they prayed for our family outside of that room and continued to pray for us for months afterwards. After much prayer and consideration, the stake appealed on our behalf to the First Presidency and requested we be allowed to attend a different ward than our geographical location dictated. The First Presidency agreed, and we were assigned to a new ward. Independent of what was happening to us, on the same day Sawyer died, there was a special stake meeting that occurred. The wards had grown and the stake was redrawing the boundaries of each congregation creating a new ward. It is that ward we were asked to attend. Some people said, "Oh, you probably got assigned there because it is a small congregation just starting out and they need people." While that may be how it looks on the outside, I do not believe that is why we were assigned there. In one of the first meetings we had with the stake presidency after Sawyer died, President Baltich said, "We know you need to heal in a different ward than you are currently attending. While we pray about where that will be, we want you to understand one thing. We are not praying for which ward will be best for you to heal in. We are praying about which bishop will be best to help heal your family." Indeed, the place we were put was exactly where we needed to be. Our new bishop had also lost child almost a decade earlier. He understood our pain in a way other people could not. He held us close. He sent us emails at difficult times, he adjusted our assignments to meet what we could handle, he helped our children acclimate to life without their brother. He did for us what the Savior needed him to do to help our family not lose our faith. It was a decision that continues to impact our family positively and another example of a tender mercy of the Lord to help us along our way, helping us maintain our testimonies and faith.

A new building with new people in a newly formed ward helped, but it didn't make church easy. The first Sunday in our new ward, a gentleman got up and talked about how he was healed after a nearly life-ending heart attack. He talked about how grateful he was for the power of prayer and how so many faithful people prayed for his recovery and again expressed his gratitude. All I could do was walk out. We all did. Our new little family walked out of sacrament meeting. We all sobbed. So, were we as a family not faithful enough for Sawyer to be healed? Were the people who gave him blessings not faithful enough? Were the wrong words said or the sins of my past coming back to me as punishment?

So often you hear the word "sorrow" coupled with the word "sin." Maybe there is some sort of guilt by association for us as disciples, I don't know. I have time and time again been told things from people of faith that do not sit well with me. Things like, "You must not understand the doctrine if you have the belief that faith and sorrow can hold the same space. We are taught life is to be joyful and we can find peace in the Atonement of Jesus Christ. If you can't find peace and happiness, you aren't being faithful enough." I have a firm testimony Christ wants us to have joy. I also believe what Shayne M. Bowen, Latter-day Saint leader, taught when he spoke directly about child loss in his talk "Because I Live, Ye Shall Live Also." I am always skeptical now when someone is speaking directly to me as someone who lost not just "a" child but *my* child, my Sawyer. Will they know what they are talking about? Do they have a sense of my devastation? Do they need what I need, and can they offer what I want to hear to comfort my aching soul? Usually not, but this time he did. He said,

> Sometimes people will ask, "How long did it take you to get over it?" The truth is, you will never completely get over it until you are together once again with your departed loved ones. I will never have a fullness of joy until we are reunited in the morning of the First Resurrection.
>
> "For man is spirit. The elements are eternal, and spirit and element, inseparably connected, receive a fulness of joy;
>
> "And when separated, man cannot receive a fulness of joy."
>
> But in the meantime, as the Savior taught, we can continue with good cheer.
>
> I have learned that the bitter, almost unbearable pain can become sweet as you turn to your Father in Heaven and plead for

*His comfort that comes through His plan; His Son, Jesus Christ; and His Comforter, who is the Holy Ghost.*

*What a glorious blessing this is in our lives. Wouldn't it be tragic if we didn't feel great sorrow when we lose a child? How grateful I am to my Father in Heaven that He allows us to love deeply and love eternally.*

Shayne M. Bowen offered me a nugget that brought me comfort to hold with my sadness. He said essentially that while the Atonement can help me and can bring me a sense of peace, complete healing will most likely not take place until I am reunited with my loved one again in the next life. Finally! Finally, something that sounded right.

So many well-intentioned believers have spouted doctrine that did nothing except alienate me to them and make me question my own beliefs. Yes, I understand the doctrine of salvation. Yes, I understand the Atonement. Yes, I hear that the spirit world is a paradise free of the evils we live in here and amongst. Yes, I know God has a plan for me and a plan for Sawyer and it doesn't look like the plan I had envisioned for us both at the moment I gave birth to him. Yes. Yes. Yes. To all of it. But my sweet baby was gone. He wasn't here to scare the crap out of me anymore. He wasn't here to torment his siblings. He wasn't here to hide sandwiches and infuriate me to no end. He wasn't here to glide magically up and down any sports field with his ability and beauty. And while all of the doctrine is in my head, my boy isn't in my life in the same way anymore, and like it or not, that changes everything. And nothing. It doesn't change my knowledge of the gospel, but it does change the way I interact with my testimony. It does change the way I hear the sacrament prayer. It does change the way I listen to every hymn and how it references death. It just does and that has to be okay. I do not need people, well intentioned and even with the proper authority, to tell me Sawyer is in a better place.

(By the way, do not say "he's in a better place" to me unless you want me to punch you in the face. Or anyone grieving the death of someone they love. I need people to love me. To tell me they don't know what to say. And to tell me they understand that I will not be completely healed until Sawyer and I are reunited and caught up on all the things we were both occupied with until that very moment.)

Reading Elder Bowen's talk changed me in my grief. It gave me permission to realize there is a part of me that cannot be whole again until I see Sawyer again, and the brokenness in me is okay! It also made me think that those who suggest being sad for too long after someone has died aren't heeding the call to comfort those who stand in need of comfort, and it isn't very Christ-like at all.

We have a friend, Martha, mother to our dear friends, who lost her husband the same year Sawyer died. That loving and devoted couple was struck by dumb cancer which resulted in earthly separation way too soon, and Martha was struggling with the passing of her eternal companion, Larry. Jack was the one who initially reached out to her. As we felt our loss compounded by the holidays, he wondered if she was feeling the same and wanted her to know she wasn't alone. It began a relationship about grieving and the gospel and discussions about the difference between knowing the doctrine of the eternal plan of salvation and missing our loved ones in a very real and daily way. She had a support network, but soon her network got busy. Those stewards assigned to look after her had young children and didn't have time to comfort a widow in the way she needed comforting. She approached her church leader and asked for someone who could come and sit with her occasionally, change a smoke detector battery, and console her with an occasional spiritual message. She was told, "Martha, it's been a *year*! What do you want from us? *You have been grieving long enough.*" Her husband had been a leader of their congregation, both of their lives spent in service to the church and its members. Yet when her time of need expanded past the delivery of funeral potatoes and a couple of mowed lawns, it was deemed too much and her grief lasting too long. If you think it is just one insensitive leader, think again.

Around the one-year mark of Sawyer's death, Grayson had started seminary, a daily scripture study class, before school started. Finn was on a mission and studying the scriptures daily. I thought, if they can, I can, and I indeed should be studying the scriptures more. I decided to attend the local scripture study class. It was a very large class, fifty or more in attendance, and it was easy to get lost in the crowd, which was my goal. However, one week the teacher started talking about the eternal nature of our lives, the plan of salvation. A tough subject for anyone to teach with *me* in the audience, but when she said from the pulpit, "It is so much easier for people who have lost a beloved spouse or child to know about the afterlife . . ." I lost it. *Easier*?! I quietly gathered my things (after composing myself as best as I could with the hyperventilating cry that was starting to creep out of my chest) and walked out. I threw my books into the car and just sat and sobbed. I didn't know the teacher well, but I do know she has not lost a spouse or a child. She did, however, know I had, and many others in the audience had lost loved ones as well. I do not think telling people how easy it is to handle loss when they have not lived it is entirely insensitive. Even though what she said may be true for some people, to hold those words in such a casual way can, and was, hurtful. Currently, I do not find knowledge of the afterlife makes things any *easier* for me. "Easy" and "loss" just don't belong in the same sentence. We have to be careful when we have the power of the pulpit about making sweeping statements and hasty generalizations. As individuals, we tend to throw these one-liners out casually to try and explain complicated doctrines and it does nothing but hurt those who don't view things in a similar way. I can understand how my high school friend lost her faith in all her grief. If you think it is just one insensitive teacher, think again.

Someone had the audacity to tell me that perhaps Sawyer died to help Grayson become a stronger person or to prepare him in some way for his future. Who would say something like that? Who? I will tell you who. Someone who has attended church all of her life and who knows the phrase "God has a plan" but who doesn't totally understand the doctrine and who clearly doesn't understand the power of her words. She was essentially suggesting Sawyer died to *teach* Grayson something?! I shook my head and in awe said nothing. The entire time we spent together, I kept trying to think of how I could address her inaccurate and incomplete understanding of the doctrine, but I didn't want to make waves. After all, I do believe most people say these sweeping comments in an attempt to make us feel better. People do not understand that these trite one-liners do not accurately reflect the depth of the ideology and instead push grievers into a corner. "Well, you do believe God has a plan, right?" Right? "So, smile because even though we don't understand The Plan, it is His Plan and therefore we should be happy, right?" Right? It is never that simple and to try and express it in such simplistic terms forces grievers to question if it is indeed okay to question The Plan. It makes grievers evaluate the quality and quantity of their faith. "Well, I do believe God has a plan for us. So, what you are basically telling me is that God planned for Sawyer to die at age ten, bringing trauma and sorrow for years to come for me and my family? And if I don't just get behind that, my faith is lacking?" It isn't that simple. Please don't pretend that it is. And if you think it is just one well-intentioned friend, think again.

Another faith-based one-liner that makes me want to punch someone is "He is in a better place now." I haven't yet, but don't be shocked if you hear on the news I eventually cave to my natural base tendencies and sock some well-intentioned believer. Here's why. Personalize it. Which of your children, spouse, loved ones would you rather have in that better place than with you right now? And no, you cannot answer your 97-year-old great grandfather who has been struggling with cancer and Alzheimer's off and on for forty years. You have to pick your new lover, your daughter newly pregnant, your son graduating with honors heading off to his successful new job, your ten-year-old just learning to navigate the world and show the world who he is going to be. You might read this and think, "No one actually says that. Sure, they might think it, but no one would say it to a mother who buried her ten-year-old son."

Think again. We were eating macaroons after finishing our greek salads. I'd mustered up the strength to attend another religion class and went to lunch afterwards with some people who were in attendance as well. A mere acquaintance said, "Tell me again what happened to your son," like she couldn't remember the color we had chosen to paint our house or the type of new car we'd purchased. "Well, [insert a gulp from holding back tears in this tiny restaurant seated with people you barely know], he died of a congenital brain malformation causing a seizure, brain swelling, and death." "Well, it's sad for you, but aren't you glad he is in a better place?" Um, no. No, I am not. I have mortal eyes and as far as my frail heart is concerned, the best place for him is here. With me, learning and growing and laughing and loving. And may I have the check please?

When our new bishop was finally brave enough to extend a calling to me, he asked me to be a teacher for the Relief Society, the women's organization in our church. It is the third hour of church when the men and women separate for personalized instruction in the gospel. I agreed. I was anxious to begin serving the Lord again in some way but was concerned with my inability to pin down any responsibility. Plus, I was feeling tentative in my faith and relationship with God who "let" this terrible thing happen, so I was concerned about jumping back in. Before, I had enjoyed teaching and liked the preparation part of the calling—reading, studying, learning the scriptures and doctrine in a more in-depth way, then finding a way to bring that to life for the sisters I worshipped with, which was something that benefitted me more than those I taught. My first lesson was tough, but I learned something important. God wanted me at church. God wanted my broken, bent, torn up, bruised testimony at church. He needed me at church. He knew that I was going to struggle with feeling betrayed and broken and needed the peace only He could bring, even though finding my way to such a peace meant fighting through a lot of messy, ugly, difficult moments I would also experience at church.

Normally, when I teach a lesson, I delete my notes. I feel like if I ever have to teach a lesson on the same subject again, I should do the research again to learn and grow and let the Spirit guide me in the direction I need to go for that particular class. But I saved this lesson. I also usually only jot down bullet points but, worried I would not be able to maintain composure, I wrote it out. I want to share a portion of it here.

*The Sunday you spent in the combined meeting about how you were going to be in this newly established ward, I was in a hospital waiting for the final surgery in which my Sawyer offered seven lifesaving gifts to children around the country. As we met with the stake presidency, the weekend we were in the hospital, they too prayed with us and over Sawyer. At that point we knew Sawyer was not coming home with us. The stake presidency was there to try and comfort us, even though we were comfortless. For several weeks after Sawyer passed, we could not go to church. We could not go anywhere. One Sunday, Jack got up and dressed with family who were still in town to go to sacrament meeting. I told him I wasn't going but was grateful he felt he could go.*

*On his way out the door, he broke down; he couldn't face it. The people, the building we last were with Sawyer in for church, the places along the road we would laugh and joke, the bench we sat on, the tree he would climb. He could face none of it. We stayed home. After another week or so we knew we needed the sacrament so we started attending a random ward just so we could partake of the sacrament. We met with the stake presidency on a couple of occasions. On one occasion we met with the stake presidency and they shared with us some very sacred experiences about answers to prayers they had been offering on our behalf. Part of the answer was that we need a new church space to heal in. The other part of it was that God was keenly aware of us as a little family unit, mourning and in pain. God was aware of us. God had Sawyer and he was safe. We attended different congregations for a few more weeks until it was official and when the official letter arrived from the First Presidency allowing us to change our records, we started attending here. Why do I share the details of how we arrived? Elder Uchtdorf's talk I have been asked to teach about is on faith. One day soon, you will hear and know my testimony. For now, I share the testimony of Elder Uchtdorf who says, "God is real. He lives. He loves you. He understands you. He knows the silent pleadings of your heart. He has not abandoned you. He will not forsake you. It is my apostolic blessing that you will feel this sublime truth for yourselves.*

I rested on this promise in the immediate weeks and months following Sawyer's death. I still do at times. I prayed and still pray for confirmation of this truth, to feel and remember God has not abandoned me. That while life and genetics and doctors and tragedy got in the way of our family plan, God did not plot and plan ways for me to suffer but He has shown me a way, a Plan, to find a way through my suffering. God Himself can't show up with a casserole or send a card. The *only way* I know He hasn't abandoned me is because He sends angels to my doorstep. Those angels are helping unbury me and find ways to sanctify myself through my tragedy.

About a month after Sawyer died, I wanted to reach out to the nurses and doctors who served us so well while we were at the hospital.

I wanted to say thank you. My mother raised me to always write thank you notes. Everyone said it was unnecessary, even a little crazy, but it was critically important to me. In part because I wanted them to see a picture of my Sawyer, not the Sawyer they saw. That wasn't my Sawyer. I also know what they did for him, and the way they did it, and I needed them to know it mattered to us. They were thoughtful, respectful, considerate of the circumstances, and prompted me to tell everyone who would listen, "At the worst time of our lives, we were surrounded by the best people." I wrote a letter expressing my feelings and I included a copy of "Agony in the Garden" (the picture we taped at the end of his bed from Brittany), and my brief, faltering, but enduring testimony. I don't know why I included my testimony in the letter. To this day, it surprises me. I am not a great missionary. I often find myself apologizing for extremists acting in the name of my faith for their shameful behavior, defending my faith to my critics who are critical for good reason. But it was important to me that everyone who didn't get to see Sawyer's life as a testimony to Sawyer's goodness and the goodness of God, at least had a chance to read that I believed it. I think I needed to write it down to remind and convince me more than sway any of the recipients. I have maintained my faith but not without a lot of work, questioning, screaming, crying, asking, doubting, and ultimately deciding I believe. And that's okay. I can hold faith and grief in the same space. I can hold faith and sadness in the same space. I can hold faith and all the other complex emotions that come with the death of my youngest son as long as I "first doubt [my] doubts before [I] doubt [my] faith" (Uchtdorf, "Come, Join with Us").

# Chapter 13

## *The Reciprocity of Service*

CHRISTMAS WAS APPROACHING. IT FELT LIKE IT HAD ONLY BEEN AN instant since Sawyer died but really it was two months later, almost to the day. We wanted to cancel Christmas and hide away until every tree was trashed and every store had disassembled the Spirit of Christmas. Well, Jack and I did, but our surviving children wanted to have Christmas. Of course they did, they were children. Even Finn, who was coming home for the break, wanted to celebrate. He'd been able to step out of the immediateness of our sadness because he'd been thrust into the school semester and was ready to come home and celebrate simply surviving college after our tragedy. Jack and I tried to salvage some semblance of Christmas for our children, but I didn't feel like decorating and couldn't feign jolly as hard as I tried. I definitely didn't want our traditions to go on as usual, or to see Sawyer's Christmas ornaments or anything else that reminded me that Sawyer would miss all of our Christmases from now on. I knew in my heart that one day I would bring out those boxes and memories but not this year. As the thick of the season settled in everywhere we went, the decorations and carols and jolly holiday vibes weren't settling well with me.

Just after dinner on December 12th, our dog Cookie started barking ferociously. Cookie is eight pounds soaking wet so she's not ferocious, but something was awry and she was on it. After putting

Cookie in another room, Jack went to the door and there was our Christmas Spirit wrapped in a nice shiny bag with this note attached:

*"Our family has chosen your family to receive our 12 Days of Christmas this year. Therefore, for the next eleven nights we will leave a gift on your front porch. We've never met you but have heard your tragic story. Our desire is to bring a smile into your day during this Christmas season. We wish to remain anonymous. Thank you for allowing us to do so. This isn't about us, it's about you."*

For the next twelve days, someone dropped goodies in pretty packages at our door every day. We later learned who it was and indeed, they were strangers. We respected their desire to remain anonymous, but every time Cookie barked, the children would get antsy waiting to see what surprise awaited them at the front door. Strangers brought the Christmas Spirit to us when we weren't able to muster it up ourselves.

A couple of days in, we all realized we wanted to do something back for our friends! We wanted them to know how grateful we were for all they had done for us. Jack baked some bread and we left them a little note of gratitude in their usual drop off spot and it made us feel so good. As the deliveries happened night after night and we saw a little twinkle start to return in the eyes of our innocent yet grief-stricken children, we got obsessed. We decided right then we wanted to do the twelve days for someone else the following year. I got really obsessed with the notion. When the after Christmas sales began, we started picking up items we could use the following year to brighten someone else's doorstep. Grieving or not, I am always interested in finding a sale rack. December 2017 rolled around and we knew exactly who we wanted to serve. As we assembled the items, we were excited about the project, but not nearly as excited as we were thinking about and planning it the prior December.

I have thought about why that was the case, why we were so driven in the thick of our grief to pull this project together, when we had an entire year to make it happen. Now I think I realize why. When we serve others, we grow closer to God, and after Sawyer died, we were desperate to feel closer to God. We were so disconnected from feelings of happiness, of joy, and of peace that the idea of serving others gave us strength. Of course, it also served as a distraction, which we needed too. Let me be clear, it wasn't much. Just small tokens to bring a smile to someone who needed it, just as we needed it. But for us, in our time of desperation, this small project was enough to remind us we would one day serve others again and enough for us to show God that we recognized the serving hands of our friends were the serving hands of God. We were in desperate need of service ourselves and we were grateful to receive it. Seeing others serve us connected us to God in a way we knew He was looking out for us, He remembered us, and He was doing what He could to send comfort our way. There was power and strength being on the receiving end of service. That said, at the time we were also feeling empty because we weren't in a position to help others. I wonder if that emptiness in the past was a feeling of pride as well. As I said before, accepting charity is just as important as offering charity, and I realized in my life I hadn't understood it was a balance and there were things to be learned on both ends. My desire to assemble my own twelve days project for an unknown stranger reminded me and my family we would again return to serve Him through others as well. It also helped teach me an important lesson about the charity of others. Neither always giving nor always receiving charity teaches me what I need to know. Rather, finding humility in both is what helps me grow to be a better person. We had been inundated with service from others. I needed to find some balance and it was simple, little gestures of giving that served to reconnect me to a God whom I loved dearly, but whom I was struggling with for taking my Sawyer way, way too soon.

. . . . . . . . . . . . . . . . . .

The walls of our house felt like they were caving in on us, and while they provided a safe haven from the onslaught of sympathetic glances, they also were starting to feel a little confining. We just needed to get out and do something. Our friends were driving through the state to pick up their daughter from college for Christmas and asked if we wanted to meet up for dinner. Reluctantly, we agreed. We wanted to be with people but weren't sure our tender hearts and volatile eyes could handle such a meeting so soon after Sawyer's death. Jack and I met them at some random Mexican restaurant in the middle of nowhere, which was perfect because we knew no one and no one knew us. Plus, the whole family has been addicted to Mexican food since, well, birth I think, and we hadn't really eaten for pleasure since Sawyer died. We needed hot sauce coursing through our veins. We ordered our sub-par enchiladas and just cried. It was the first time we'd been out of the house with anyone without an expressly grief-related purpose, though we were experts in recognizing that everything was at least subtly grief related. The dinner was nice because good friends were letting us cry and eat and talk and eat and cry and eat some more without judgment which is exactly what we needed. But time passed and we needed to return home to our children, so we said goodbye and headed home.

Our meeting spot was about 90 minutes from home, so halfway to our destination, Jack pulled over to put gas in the car. As we were pulling out, he noticed a car near the air pump with several people milling about. I told him we didn't have time to help, it was late, the kids needed us home and the babysitter needed to be sent home, not to mention we were a hot mess ourselves. (Yeah, that didn't fly.) He went over and asked if anything was wrong and if he could help. Long story, but it involved a baby delivery, kids out past bedtime, lack of food, and really cold temperatures with no coats. He offered our warm car for waiting passengers, rolled up his sleeves, and started to troubleshoot with the owner. I waited in the car, grateful for the uninterrupted time to disconnect from my troubles and watch something on my phone. After about an hour, there was nothing more he could do, and it was evident they were going to have to call a service. As we drove away, Jack started to cry. I asked why he was crying, and he said, "It just felt so good to try and help someone instead of being the one needing help. Haven't felt that in a while." There was no grand gesture, we weren't ultimately able to help them, but we were willing to try, and it felt good.

. . . . . . . . . . . . . . . . . . .

I've mentioned before that Jack likes to connect with his school personnel at work on a personal level whenever he can. He always has been, and I imagine always will be, a people person. He finds commonalities first whereas I tend to find differences first. After "Thursday" but before Christmas, a teacher's aide at the elementary school in the county experienced a somewhat similar tragedy to our own. Her adult son was driving home from work and was in a fatal car accident. The community couldn't believe yet another one of our youth was happy and healthy one day and in an instant was gone. As we were still reeling ourselves from Sawyer's death, I told him he didn't need to go to her house. He said, "Because of Sawyer, I have to go now more than ever."

I hate to admit it most days, but clearly I married up. He went over and brought a couple of gallons of ice cream with him, which was something we appreciated when someone had done it for us after Sawyer died. At that moment she wasn't an employee, she was another grieving parent. She opened the door and said, "What are you doing here? I never expected you would come, you know, because . . ." Yes, he knew.

. . . . . . . . . . . . . . . . . .

For months before Sawyer died, all the boys, including and probably most especially Jack, had been hearing about the new Nintendo Entertainment System (NES). It was coming out for the Christmas season and was sure to be a hot item. All the boys were excited about trying to get their hands on one for Christmas and the plan was to play all day and all night over break. Finn was to be home and it was going to be a family game-a-thon. Then Sawyer died and we all lost interest in everything from before. Almost everything. Jack became obsessed with getting his hands on one of these systems and with each passing day, the prospect of landing one got more and more bleak, which of course fueled Jack even more. "We have lost so much, I'm not going to let the boys lose this too." Again, a seemingly simple material possession represented so much more to our family. I will spare you the details of how he got his hands on one, but he did. As soon as it was in his hot little hands, he called and asked, "Where are you right now? GameStop has three. Literally only three. Come buy another one right now so we can give it to Finn to take back to college with him." Just what every freshman taking junior level engineering classes needs, a distraction. On a total fluke, I was close, so I ran over and managed to get my hands on the second system. "I just sold the first of the three and now the second within minutes," said the cashier. Yep, you did, and we thank you for it.

We were actually energized. We felt a small sense of excitement we would be able to give this to the boys for Christmas. Of course we cried as we drove home with the prize in our hands knowing Sawyer was so excited to play the games of his parents' youth with his brothers. Again, grief and happiness occupying the same space was a concept and adjustment we were still navigating. Add the sheer joy of this moment to the list of things we *lost*.

You know that about grief, right? It isn't just the person or thing you lost that disappears, but an endless list of seemingly unrelated things disappear too. Obviously, they don't hold the same value, it's just the notion of one enormous loss, compounded by a litany of smaller losses, adding insult to injury. And since I've already started down this path, can I go off a minute? I hate saying the word "lost" when we refer to Sawyer because that implies control on our part. When you lose your keys, it means you did something and now the keys are gone. I did nothing other than birth him to cause his death. He wasn't lost. Anyway, rant over.

Here are some examples of our seemingly unrelated losses: Grayson lost our game room as a space to hang out because it was too painful to be in there without Sawyer. I lost my van, which I adored, as a fun memory keeper. Jack lost the magic of sushi and Japanese soda. Finn lost a breezy freshman year at college. We all lost frozen burritos, theme parks, and the beach. Sterling lost a lifetime with Sawyer. Jack's friend, who was in the middle of his divorce, lost all of the obvious things a divorce brings, but also foods, places, events, people. Everyone grieving suffers an infinite amount of corollary losses. One I talk about often is my love of reading. Before Sawyer died, I was in multiple book groups wherever I lived. Trying to get the energy to pick up a book, let alone finish it, was impossible for me for a long time after Sawyer died. Never mind the complexity of words on a page, ideas in a chapter, but I swear every book in the world that has any sort of veneration includes something about death. (Present company included.) I was dealing with my own tragedy, I didn't need to read about someone else's and relive my tough emotions when I had previously used reading as an escape. It's like I hadn't learned Sawyer's death was inescapable. Sorrow bleeds into every aspect of your life. Okay, sidebar over. Anyway, the children would get their NES. Plus, we had an extra one for Finn.

One of the angels who helped us in our sorrow is Daniel Woodfin. He was the funeral director at the crematorium we used for Sawyer. Daniel's story is unique. He was in sales before his job at the crematorium. His father passed away unexpectedly several years earlier. His dad was out in his yard raking leaves and had a heart attack, and when his family found him, he was dead. His family then proceeded to wait almost thirteen hours with their deceased father in their front yard before the mortuary came to take his body to the funeral home. Thirteen hours his family sat vigil with him in shifts in the yard. Daniel was so disgusted with how his father and subsequently his entire family was treated that he decided then and there he was going to make sure no other family endured such hell at the worst time of their life. His career detoured and he went back to be trained for three years to be able to serve people in this capacity. He was there for us in private, tender, sacred moments and he honored our sweet boy in so many ways. One of the ways he served us was in coming to our house to transfer Sawyer's remains from the temporary urn when the final urn we had made for him arrived at our house. "No parent should have to touch their son's ashes, I will do it for you." That wasn't the final service he provided for our family, he continually did kind things for us as difficult situations arose.

The day we got the NES games was the day Daniel came to our home to put Sawyer's ashes in their final resting place. He came into the house and saw the games. "Oh, that is so cool you got those! I want one so badly for my boys but can't find one anywhere. I am thinking of taking a day off work next week to go try and wait in line a couple places." While he was out in our garage that day doing a task we knew we couldn't do for ourselves, Jack and I looked at the NES games and then at each other. Without saying it, we knew we would be giving one of them to Daniel. (Finn's of course . . . sorry Finn!) Daniel was ever so grateful and offered to pay us and we politely declined. When we told a friend about the exchange, she said, "You could have at least had him pay you for it. Getting his hands on it was the gift." No amount of money could repay him for the service he provided to our family in such a loving and respectful way. His kindness and generosity was something we knew we could never give back to him to the same degree. There are sacred parts of our family story that no one will know, yet Daniel witnessed. Here was this tiny way we could give back to him and it felt good.

. . . . . . . . . . . . . . . . . .

You'll notice in these examples, Jack was the impetus igniting our service. I was hesitant. I was feeling self-absorbed, and rightly so, I believe. But Jack was willing to step out of our fog to help others and as he would lead the way, I was willing to follow. I think sometimes if we don't have the idea ourselves, we are reluctant to jump in and get involved. I found that when I couldn't see clearly enough to look around to acknowledge others in need, acting on nudges we felt to help others served as a lifeline for us both. Our life as a family has been extremely blessed. We have been fortunate for most of our lives to be on the giving end of service. But in that, we have also been missing out on the blessing of receiving with grace and the humility it can bring. I don't share our little stories of service to boast (I mean look, we weren't moving mountains or curing diseases), but I share them because they were little acts of service we could perform within the bounds of our grief and sadness. They were offerings that, albeit small and inconsequential to those on the other side, helped us find a sense of balance again.

There are seasons for everything, we are told. With exceptions of course, my family has been in the position to accept calls to have a meal delivered, a ride for someone to the doctor, a blessing for someone who was sick, a friendly face for a lonely, disenfranchised member at church or in the community. Receiving an abundance of service when Sawyer died in such a profound and exhaustive way was new to us and we at times struggled with it. Accepting service taught us to overcome our pride and to learn more about the notion of grace. We were able to actually find some quiet moments of peace and reflection because of the service rendered to us. Somewhere in the middle of all of our grief and sadness and coping and healing, we learned an important lesson about the seasons of giving and the equally important seasons of receiving.

I have learned that in life we can "take" something that is offered to us but not necessarily "receive" it. There can be a spirituality almost in the way in which we accept the service rendered us by others. Following Sawyer's death, for us, there became a sort of sacredness in receiving help from other people. It taught us acceptance of others in a way we had never known, particularly as we watched people who were important in our lives come to us in their own tears and share a story of their own grief. It taught us humility in a way we had never experienced before as we saw strangers deliver goodness and smiles to our doorstep in many different forms. We learned compassion as we watched people, in the midst of their own storms, step into our storm to help us weather it. And in all of their service, we felt the hand of God. Understanding and seeing that side of charity is humbling and it also impressed on me the importance of both sides of the coin, and finding balance in both offering and accepting service in all forms. There must be reciprocity of service. We must give, we must receive. We must learn both sides if we are to truly become empathetic and be able to relate and serve those around us. For me, in my grief, I was able to experience this in powerful ways and it helped me find power and strength in acknowledging the giving and receiving.

# Chapter 14

# The "Bereaved Sibling"

(Or, in less clinical speak, *"Gear up, your childhood will never be the same."*)

STERLING HAS A REOCCURRING DREAM THAT ALWAYS RESULTS IN HER waking up screaming and in tears. If we are lucky enough to be asleep when it happens, it jars us from our slumber, but usually one of us is up and stewing anyway. We run in, ask her what's wrong, and she tells us her dream, again. To the world, the dream is fairly benign, which is part of what makes it so painful for all of us. She dreams that Sawyer is over at a friend's house and he comes home. She wakes up and realizes he isn't at a friend's house and he is never coming home. She first had the dream a few weeks after Sawyer died and we thought it would eventually subside, but here we are just over a year later and it happened again last night. Pain from Sawyer's death is pervasive, and it is particularly powerful in relation to all of Sawyer's siblings. His death had an immediate impact on them, and we are now seeing the clear impact it is having on the trajectory of their lives. This is not hyperbole.

If you ask Sterling to tell you a story or memory about Sawyer, it is always the same. "Remember that time Sawyer farted in my face? It was disgusting! I almost barfed." It is the first story that comes to her mind and she repeats it regularly. If you ask Grayson to tell you a story about Sawyer, he will hem and haw and deflect. He isn't ready to openly speak about his best friend and brother dying. If you ask Finn to tell you a Sawyer story, he will smile, tear up, and appear a little overwhelmed because there are so many to choose from, but he will always launch into one. Of course, every child is different and every child grieves in their own way, just like adults. Dealing with the grief of a child dying, and I would submit dealing with any loss or tragedy, is so complicated and foreign to most of us that having to help your children cope with such a tragedy compounds the already complicated. At least it was for me anyway. I felt like I was barely surviving, but I knew I could not curl up and die myself, even though I wanted to, because I needed my children to come out of this life-changing tragedy heartbroken, but not broken. And I had no idea how I was supposed to make that happen.

In the hospital, the hospice nurses handled much of the difficult discussions with Sterling, but we had discussions about death with Finn and Grayson ourselves. We were so consumed though; we left a lot of the talking for when we were home from the hospital after Sawyer died. Grayson and Finn, devastated, knew exactly what was going on and felt every sorrowful moment with us. Sterling, as a four-year-old, really couldn't grasp everything that was happening, nor did we expect her to. We needed to come up with a narrative we felt was spiritually in line with our beliefs but that also was age appropriate. My grandmother had passed earlier in the year and Grandma Meacham was known, even to little Sterling, for her triple layer chocolate cream cheese cake. We sat Sterling down and talked with her about Sawyer dying. The counselors all said it was important to use the words "death" and "died" with her because other euphemisms create confusion for children. We talked about the sad truth that Sawyer had died and his spirit was in heaven with Grandma Meacham and they were having a big party there, probably enjoying her triple layer cake. When Sterling later asked when Sawyer was coming back from heaven, we knew we had blown it. The concept of an afterlife is complicated for adults to process, never mind a four-year-old who had an immediate need to understand. In that moment I knew this was going to be a long process of understanding and teaching and acknowledging. I also knew there were going to be more mistakes made and it became my prayer that my mistakes would not scar my children any more than having their brother die already had.

Daniel Woodfin, our angel from the funeral home, did something amazing for our children. When my father-in-law, Bob, went to pick up Sawyer's ashes, Daniel had sent Sawyer's photograph off to a company to have a quilt made showcasing Sawyer's smiling face, his beautifully jacked up teeth still approaching the braces phase, and some of Sawyer's interests. The quilt was a lovely gesture and now sits on a chair in our living room and will sit there until the day I die. When Bob brought it home, we cried and we also laughed. It was a little comical to us because it was a ginormous photo of Sawyer and a crazy cat with sunglasses on it, something Sawyer would have loved, and for some reason set off the giggles in us. We weren't sure what to do with the quilt initially. Do we hang it on a wall to display? Do we wrap ourselves up in it? Do we toss it in the car to bring Sawyer along for picnics? We were learning how to handle and respond to what we refer to as our "grief swag." One afternoon, Grayson was sitting in our big, oversized leather chair and had the Sawyer blanket on top of him. Sterling walked by Grayson and the blanket with a plate of food, I don't remember what it was, but I remember as she was walking by, I held my breath in, nervous she would spill. "Sterling, please go eat in the kitchen. We don't eat in the living room and I don't want food near the Sawyer blanket. I want to keep it in good condition, please." (I'm sure I said it just like that, right? Polite and calm and loving . . .) She went into the kitchen, set down her plate and returned with a glass of water which, before I could say anything, was spilled all over Grayson and the blanket as she tripped on the rug.

I freaked out in the weirdest of ways. In a heartbeat I said, "Sterling, you owe Sawyer an apology, you spilled all over his blanket." Then I started to laugh because that made no sense and then all three of us started to cry hysterically. We knew the blanket wasn't Sawyer. We knew it was threads woven together to represent Sawyer. But we had a hard time not transferring our feelings for Sawyer to all the things that represented Sawyer. That would be and continues to be my challenge as a mother: to help my children build a new relationship with their brother who was no longer here and wouldn't be back. And how in the world was I, of all people, supposed to do that?

I crowdsourced my concern to social media hoping surely some-one would be able to teach me something. One thing I did learn after Sawyer died is that sadly a lot of our collective friends had lost a sibling at some point either in their childhood or as an adult and they had a lot to say about it, when asked. Most of these friends hadn't previously disclosed their experiences with the death of their sibling until it was relevant to us. It has made me think a lot about the way we do or don't offer our friends opportunities to share their grief. I know it's not great party conversation, "So have you experienced the death of a sibling or what?" I get it. It's delicate. Believe me, I get it. I just wonder if, as I build relationships in my life, do I find or make opportunities for my friends to share their grief as needed? Anyway, our friends had many powerful words to share, sadly, most surrounded the notion that my children would have to live and pass through this grief and find their own way out, guided by me as their mother. There was no real answer. One theme I did hear repeatedly was, "We weren't allowed to (or just never did) talk about my sibling after they died. It was just too painful for my parents. So, we just sort of moved on and closed that chapter of our life." It broke my heart to hear this sentiment over and over again, but I completely understood it! Every time Sterling opened her mouth, we were all on edge won-dering if she was going to tell another Sawyer story. While we loved hearing them, they broke our heart in new places every time. It was something I knew we needed to power through.

But grief never makes sense and what is good for one, isn't always good for another. Sterling freely shared Sawyer stories and we would watch Grayson as she would tell her stories and he would tear up or walk away. It was too much. Closing down this chapter of our life and moving on without Sawyer was not an option. There was a harsh real-ity we had to face, and it was harsh because it was so true. Grayson's childhood was over at thirteen. Sawyer's death cemented that truth. Sterling's life with Sawyer was over and probably, because she was so young, would eventually turn to a soft memory in the back of her heart but wouldn't be the ever-present relationship we'd always envi-sioned. From early on, we joked about how Sterling and Sawyer were so similar that once Grayson eventually moved out of the house, the two of them were going to cause quite a stir, which is code for *get in a lot of trouble together.* Maintaining Sawyer's relationship in a new way with his siblings became my mission, albeit almost impossible. I came across a poem by Henry Scott Holland entitled "Death is Nothing at All" and it became my lifeline and guidebook for parenting my grieving children and keeping Sawyer present.

*Death is nothing at all.*
*It does not count.*
*I have only slipped away into the next room.*
*Nothing has happened.*

*Everything remains exactly as it was.*
*I am I, and you are you,*
*and the old life that we lived so fondly together is untouched,*
*unchanged.*
*Whatever we were to each other, that we are still.*

*Call me by the old familiar name.*
*Speak of me in the easy way which you always used.*
*Put no difference into your tone.*
*Wear no forced air of solemnity or sorrow.*

*Laugh as we always laughed at the little jokes that we enjoyed*
*together.*
*Play, smile, think of me, pray for me.*
*Let my name be ever the household word that it always was.*
*Let it be spoken without an effort, without the ghost of a*
*shadow upon it.*

*Life means all that it ever meant.*
*It is the same as it ever was.*
*There is absolute and unbroken continuity.*
*What is this death but a negligible accident?*

*Why should I be out of mind because I am out of sight?*
*I am but waiting for you, for an interval,*
*somewhere very near,*
*just round the corner.*

*All is well.*
*Nothing is hurt; nothing is lost.*
*One brief moment and all will be as it was before.*
*How we shall laugh at the trouble of parting when we meet again!*

I both loved and hated this poem. Because "death wasn't nothing at all"—death was everything! And yet there was a hope, a security, a sense of comfort that came from the notion that we all desperately needed. Maybe it could be our approach to building a new relationship. I didn't know. There was so, so much I didn't know.

In our house, we say prayers both audibly as a family and silently to ourselves, depending on the occasion. The first time I said a prayer out loud as a family after Sawyer died, we were all standing in the kitchen. I can envision it perfectly even now as I type. When I pray aloud, I always pray for everyone in the family individually by name and as I went through the line, it was time to pray over Sawyer. I paused. I cried. I resumed and added him to my prayer and instantly realized that wasn't going to work for a while. It was too painful to say his name in prayer and realized we weren't praying for him per se, and it was too painful to say everyone's name and skip Sawyer, so my prayers as a parent changed because of his relationship with his siblings. I prayed for Sawyer and about him when I was by myself because it hurt us all, especially Grayson, when I did it out loud. It hurt me not to pray for him, but I had to find balance and I had to respect what Grayson needed. Sterling liked to include Sawyer in her prayers and in her everyday conversation, but it was tough to hear. Life in general became a dance of how to include Sawyer and his memory in our lives so we didn't ignore Sterling's need to have him present and Grayson's need to have some healing space. Some days I thought we were handling it well, others not so much.

One day Sterling came out of her room crying particularly hard and I asked her what was wrong. She said, "I broke Sawyer's ball. When he gets back from heaven, he is going to be so mad at me." No matter what we said, books we read, or analogies we used, heaven to her four-year-old mind was no different than Florida. Her sadness coupled with our sadness and her brothers' sadness brought an overwhelming sorrow that was nearly impossible to carry. How grateful I am for shock and the accompanying numbness it brought, otherwise I am not sure any of us would have been able to make it through those early days and weeks.

I knew that my new task in life was to allow this unbearable tragedy to sanctify me rather than destroy me. This was no small task, especially when I felt so ill prepared. I also knew, however, that no matter what happened to me, it was my new task as a mother to make stronger, more empathetic, more loving children from the depths of our sorrow, rather than let it destroy us.

The task of getting the older boys back to school wasn't easy. Finn left for college right after Sawyer's Celebration of Life and he was met with all sorts of challenges. Technically an adult, he was forced to navigate much of his grieving, balanced with his classes, on his own. We did what we could from afar and he had a huge support network in the form of his friends, church congregation, and dorm room floor. His professors, for the most part, were helpful. He did have one professor who was unwilling to budge in regards to work due while he was back home to say a final goodbye to his younger brother and attend his Celebration of Life. In the end, the lack of help from this one professor in this one class did impact his grades and he lost his scholarship over it. Losing his brother wasn't enough? In the name of people not understanding grief, I have decided that the professor didn't understand the impact of grief and grieving. In the name of compassion, I have decided that the appeals department doesn't understand grief and its impact on the brain and on the heart. Finn was supposed to get a job to help pay for living expenses, but now with this weight, we knew he would be unable to keep his grades up in his rigorous classes and get a job. Learning about the scholarship loss only compounded Finn's stress. Jack and I again told him not to worry, we would help assume those extra expenses. Grief charges an emotional price but there is also a physical cost to grief and grieving and it isn't cheap. I will be forever proud of the dignity in which Finn handled everything in stride and still came out with a 3.92 GPA the semester after Sawyer's death. I believe having left the house to begin adulthood just two short months prior to Sawyer's death helped give Finn a distance, but definitely not a pass, from the day-to-day trauma of coping with his brother dying. I hope one day Finn will write a book about grief from his perspective and experience. I hope college professors and student services will get training on grief, grieving, and the impact on the brain and behavior of students and find ways to couple such knowledge with compassion and accommodations.

Grayson, on the other hand, was spared nothing. He had to sit through each painstaking moment at the hospital. Grayson had to go home without his brother. Grayson had to return to the empty bedroom he and Sawyer shared. The school they attended together. The friends they overlapped. Grayson took the biggest hit amongst the surviving siblings. I say that, but then I also backpedal a little bit. They all had their own trials and none of them had it easy. Grayson just had the most obvious impact. He didn't go back to school for several weeks and, when he did, it was a disaster. Thankfully his peers at school had been counseled and they let him have his space and didn't press him to talk about his feelings. I wonder sometimes though if he was given too much space.

There is no handbook for handling these kinds of situations, especially for teenagers. The school tried but they were ill-equipped to handle Grayson in his grief. People did not have enough empathy, understanding, and background in handling grief and it was evident almost immediately upon Grayson returning to school. One day as he was going through his schedule, he made the comment in class which the teacher heard, "Wait, March is after February?" Well of course it is. But a teacher had been discussing testing dates and everything was all jumbled in his mind. Time didn't make sense anymore to any of us and it passed/stood still at any given moment. The teacher called him out in front of the class and told him to stop being such a clown, that obviously March came after February. He came home in tears, "Mom, I swear I didn't realize what month it was. I wasn't trying to cause trouble, I just literally lost track of time. Everything is so messed up in my mind." It wasn't the only example of teachers unable to recognize his behaviors and performance were directly related to the death of his best friend and brother. We talked about pulling him out of school but feared the complete isolation would be worse. Literally, every day after school for the rest of the year, Grayson would hop in the car at our new pick up location across the street and the tears would just start to flow. I physically could not sit in the old carpool line, it was just too painful, so even the littlest of things had to change for us. Sometimes Grayson's tears would be gentle tears of gladness he actually survived the day without breaking down in front of his classmates. Sometimes they would be tears of anger and frustration that the day was filled with too much to deal with, Sawyer wasn't around, and it was all too overwhelming to handle. It broke my heart and no matter how much we tried to communicate our concern to the school, they simply didn't have the time or resources or know how to address Grayson's grief. To this day, I say if I weren't an old lady I would go back to school and become a grief counselor for teenagers. They are going through so much already developmentally at that age, to add the weight of grief on to them is almost unbearable. A dying sibling or parent, a parent in jail, homelessness, mental health, suicidal tendencies, all of it is too much for teenagers to deal with on their own, yet from where I was sitting, that was exactly what we were asking them to do. At least that's what the world was asking Grayson to do and it broke my heart. One day I hope Grayson will write about the sweet relationship he and Sawyer shared for ten years and how losing that relationship changed him. I hope school systems will aim to become trauma informed systems, actually getting some training on grief, grieving, and the impact on the brain and behavior of students and find ways to couple such knowledge with compassion and accommodations.

Finn and Grayson have so many experiences related to their grief to share but they are not mine to offer here. I've shared what limited scope I have with their permission just to offer some insight into our grieving family. So many times we were approached about how we were doing but there were very few people who asked or worried about our children. To those who reached out to our children, thank you. It made a huge difference. There were people who had children who had grown up with Grayson who I really wish would have been able to help their children reach out to him. It's an almost impossible request, I understand. Who wants to expose their children to sadness and mortality? I am not sure I would. I just know it could have really been a game changer for Grayson to have a support network of his peers. I offer this merely as something to consider if you have teenagers who know someone who is grieving. Alas, I want to write more about the horribly insensitive things people said to or about our grieving children, but I won't because they aren't mine to share. Just know that when a family is grieving, the entire family is grieving. Children and teenagers need special attention, apart from the attention of the adults and when our children got such attention, it made a huge difference.

What kind of attention? Of course, that depends on the individual child. I will say, the only way to know is to ask and not assume. We did have people who sent small gifts, usually in memoriam but also serving as a distraction, which helped the children cope. People offered to take Sterling on outings to distract her, which was the perfect way to address her needs. One of Jack's college roommates took brownies to Finn at school and my Aunt Wendy attended one of Finn's performances, all helping him feel he wasn't alone in his grieving or his healing. And while Grayson's needs were largely forgotten by his schoolteachers and church leaders, I will offer one ray of hope we experienced with Grayson. We had friends of the family who both had a child in Grayson's class and they approached us and said, "We don't know what to tell our boys in regards to how to help Grayson, but we have talked with them. We have asked them to be patient with Grayson and offer him love and acceptance no matter how he responds." This gesture gave me a sense that even if it wasn't everyone, Grayson did have people on his side, and we would all figure this out somehow. Sawyer's army would help carry us.

. . . . . . . . . . . . . . . . .

Sterling had a boy in her preschool class named Sawyer. Talk about unfortunate timing. We would sit at the dinner table and Sterling would start in about, "Sawyer <insert crazy antic here>" and we would have to process in our minds, as she was telling the story, if her story was about our Sawyer or preschool Sawyer. It turned my stomach the first several times it happened and then, like most of our sorrow journey, became something we just learned to handle.

Grayson and Sterling were each learning how to navigate their feelings about Sawyer in their own ways and it looked different for both of them publicly and privately. And if you think adults don't have the skill set to handle other grieving adults, you can imagine how little they were able to deal with children who were grieving. Adults often found it easier to ignore our children or just pretend nothing had happened when dealing with them. It was sad to witness and all I wanted was for someone other than Jack and I, who were struggling ourselves, to reach out to our children, especially Finn and Grayson, who needed strong adult role models. Here is my call to action. If you are a teacher or leader who works with youth, and a family you know experiences some sort of trauma, please, with parents' permission, reach out to those you have influence over. Build a relationship with those youth so they know that when they need you, you are there to listen or to help. It would have made a huge impact on the healing journey of my children if more adults in their lives stepped in to lend a helping hand with them, and not just us as parents.

As part of my dedication to speaking Sawyer's name, allowing Sterling to speak his name, and even encouraging it, I started to write the brief snippets Sterling, and very rarely Grayson, offered during the first year after Sawyer died. I hope by sharing them with you, I can paint another layer on the picture of the sadness of a child as reflected by their intense love and offer you a sense of the absolute need for compassion and empathy for grievers, especially grieving siblings. Death, or really any tragedy, isn't just something you experience and then it is over. It is something you deal with every single day in powerful and painful ways. I exhort you to remember such compassion when called upon to interact with those struggling with sorrow, especially children and teenagers, no matter what the cause.

I was out of my league and was thrust into parenting children dealing with trauma, tragedy, death, and the general sadness of the reality of life on earth not being all rainbows and unicorns. There are studies and books about resilience and coping and they are written by experts, of which I am not. I read them and continue to read them. Some of them are helpful and some of them are clearly written by people who have no sense or experience with grief. All I am trying to say is that we all need to try and understand children who are grieving a little better. We should assume an obligation to step into their grief with them a little bit instead of brushing it aside and pretending there is nothing wrong. Sterling's friend's mother let her talk about Sawyer, talk about him to her and to her own young child. It was a gift to have a source for progress and healing instead of just another adult who was uncomfortable broaching the subject. When something happens that triggers one of my children, they feel a version of that hurt all over again.

I got a call that Sterling had been crying in the library, so her teacher pulled her out of the class and allowed her to be a helper for the hour. She asked if Sterling wanted to talk about it and she declined. Later that evening I spoke to Sterling and got her to open up a little bit. The book they were reading as a class in the library had the title character leaving class in an ambulance because her appendix ruptured. The character got better and all her classmates cheered. Sawyer did not get better. It was a huge trigger for Sterling that the teacher acknowledged, in spite of not totally understanding, and it mattered.

I got another call (I really, at this point, wanted to stop answering all phone calls, not just the ones from the school nurse). It was Grayson's English teacher. She was preparing her lesson plan for the following day and realized they were about to start a book where the title character deals with the death of his parents. She hadn't connected the dots but in a last-minute impression, she was touched that it might trigger Grayson in ways he wasn't yet ready to handle publicly with his classmates. She asked what I thought. I first teared up at her sensitivity, thanked her, and politely asked if he could read another book in the library and do a self-paced unit. I didn't think Grayson was ready to handle such heavy emotions with the world watching. She immediately insisted she was going to change the unit, she had others to offer to the whole class, and there was no need for Grayson to feel any more outcast or "other" than he already felt amongst his peers. Everyone knew what happened to Sawyer, most watched the ambulance pull away. This teacher was willing to change her entire lesson plan for the next several weeks to accommodate Grayson in his grief. I have been critical of those who did nothing, or even done hurtful things in the wake of my children experiencing their brother dying. I also want to acknowledge those who stood up, put themselves out there, inconvenienced themselves, and sought to help my children in their pain. It makes me reflect on every past interaction I have had with a young person and I can't help but start to process all the ways

I could have been a more empathetic leader, teacher, and—painfully, frankly—mother.

Voicing all of these "should," "would," "could" statements of course doesn't stop me from thinking about all my own could haves, would haves, and should haves of the past ten years. Why do we all do that to ourselves when tragedy strikes? The phrase "hindsight is 20/20" doesn't exist in a vacuum. We can see situations differently from the perspective of being past it. As a parent, I think there are a lot of things I would do differently if I could go back. Kudos to those who think they wouldn't. I wasn't a perfect parent, and I would love to go back and give Sawyer that gift, the perfect parent. Not just Sawyer, all of my children. But I can't. But one thing I wouldn't change is all of the ways we let Sawyer live in his daredevil ways. I wouldn't try to intercede or quash his adventurous spirit in the name of safety. It is who he was and I would never want his personality altered from who I loved as a son and who his siblings loved as a brother. I now just try, with the three children I am still raising here on earth, to be in the moment. To be present. To understand that while I cannot give them a perfect parent, I can maybe give them a better parent. I try to make decisions based on the whole picture of who they are as an individual and not what seems best by the standards of the world. I try harder to be more patient. I try to say yes more or find better alternatives to no, even when saying no is so much easier. I try to compromise more. I try to ascertain what is best for them and who they are trying to become and give them opportunities to grow towards their futures. (Note to Self: Re-read these sentences when Grayson wants to wear shorts and no coat in 15-degree weather and Sterling will not let me braid her hair for school!) Their future does not involve having Sawyer here with them to play with, laugh with, live with, love with, and even fight with and I hate that reality. But as I work to bring Sawyer's memory into our daily life and let it impact the way each of my children live, I am grateful for those in my life who help supplant my efforts with efforts of their own.

One Sunday after church when I had spoken publicly about Sawyer, a woman who was new to our congregation came up to me. She introduced herself to me and asked me my son's name. She said, "I look forward to hearing more about Sawyer and getting to know about who he was as a child." I was stopped in my tracks. (Textbook people, it was textbook!) I teared up and was grateful for the interaction. For weeks afterwards I thought, "What would my children do if they were given the opportunity to talk to someone who knew Sawyer had died and who also knew how important he was to each of them?" How could my children have been helped if one of their leaders or teachers were to approach them and ask such a daring, possibly uncomfortable question like, "Would you ever want to talk to me about Sawyer?" Or maybe would have pulled them aside for time alone to process a question like that over ice cream or a walk in the park? I hope someday someone will ask such a question to each of them and they will be able to answer with loving resolve. I fear a huge part of the reservation in addressing grief with children is our own fear as adults rooted in our inability to handle and deal with grief ourselves. We as adults need to abandon the secrecy and shame associated with grief if we ever have a chance of helping grieving children.

# Chapter 15

# *The Coping*

"So I understand this is your first time, correct?" my new therapist asked.

"Yes, I am a newbie."

"Well, I want you to know everyone here at the office was deeply saddened by the news of Sawyer's passing and we extend our condolences."

"Thank you."

"Well, since you are new, let's start with something simple. What was the date Sawyer passed away?"

I started crying inconsolably. Not just because the magic of my life had vanished into seemingly thin air, but because of the mess in my mind and the complexity of how everything went down, because of how now nothing was simple anymore, and how nothing will ever be simple again, I didn't have an answer for her. My mind started racing.

Does she want the date I got *the* call? I was standing in my work-out clothes pumping gas on my way to my first meeting with the personal trainer I'd hired. Sterling was at preschool, so it was that Wednesday (right?) when I peeked at my phone and saw all the missed calls and text messages:

*Jaime pick up the phone.*

*Jaime where are you, answer your phone!*

*Jaime there is an emergency with Sawyer!*
*I am in the ambulance with Sawyer. CALL ME!*

Does she want the date of the day we heard that after three brain surgeries for Sawyer, if he made it, he would be brain dead? Let's see. I was still in my clothes, no, I had showered in that horrible hospital room shower, so it must have been that Thursday.

Does she want the date of the day the state of Virginia declared he was dead, which could only be declared after a series of tests followed by the same tests administered twelve hours later? After the intern told us about the AVM and the neurologist told us they were going to remove some of his skull? No, wait, that was before. Was it when we were told if he did survive, he wouldn't be the same, he wouldn't be our Sawyer? Was it the same day? No, we had everyone say their goodbyes at that point so it must have been that Friday. The official date. Friday, October 28, 2:38 p.m.

Does she want the date of the day we decided to donate his organs? Or rather the day the transplant coordinator arrived for her twenty-four-hour shift? Or when the second coordinator arrived for his twenty-four-hour shift? Or when our third coordinator arrived for his twenty-four-hour shift?

Does she want the date of the day of the actual organ recovery surgery, which, due to the complicated process of gathering multiple surgical teams from around the country to gather at one time, happened to be three days after the state of Virginia said he had died, but was then the date we walked out of the hospital without our son?

When did Sawyer "die"?

Remember how I said nothing was simple anymore? I wasn't lying.
    In every trauma, tragedy, and trial we all experience, I think almost everyone wants to be strong, wants to come out on top. For the few who do not, I am sorry for the gloom they must feel. That said, the rest of us try to survive in our grief, plus maintain our lives

with the hope of eventually thriving, having a lot to juggle and are often ill-equipped. At least I was (and am most days) but here we go. The people we were all used to turning to for help were also not equipped to help us. First off, our children turned to us, and we felt broken. We turned to our close friends and family who were also feeling broken. Plus, they were far away and they weren't really versed in helping others grieve. Of course, they have seen their fair share of sadness and grief, hasn't everyone? But I think coping with grief is something we do, in private, right? "Let them grieve in private," we've all said it. But in our private circle, we had no one to help us know what to do or how to survive living life without our Sawyer. Our first aid responders were awesome, in the beginning, because they were there to help put the band-aids on. They fed us, physically made sure we showered, arranged details, distracted the children when they needed distracting, sent us things, stopped by to give hugs, all of it. But soon enough, everyone needed to go back to their life, including our first responders, which meant we were left to pick up the pieces and try and figure out what to do with them; the tiny, shattered, impossible to clean up pieces that had become our life.

Think about when you have broken a dish or something similar. Sometimes you can glue the pieces back together easily, the breaks confining themselves to major cracks or fixable chips. Think about when you last broke a glass. When I had three young children, I gave all my glassware to Goodwill after watching each child mindlessly toss one in the sink where it would shatter. Glass flies everywhere, it gets stuck in the rugs, under the vent, slits in the counter, across the room, even in my hair once. The pieces are almost always impossible to retrieve in their entirety and every time we broke a glass it seemed like, at least at my house, we stepped on small shards of glass for weeks afterwards. That is what our grief felt like, still feels like. Just when we thought we had things under control, something would bubble up and a new cut requiring a new band aid would appear. It wasn't for just one of us either, this was the case for all of us.

I've already mentioned we tried traveling, and that helped, but was unrealistic as a perpetual coping strategy. We went away as often as we could, and everything people did to help support us in that was amazing. Even the trips, both long and far away and short and close by, were laced with sadness, but there was less of it when we were in new places. After a while, and after talking to many people in similar situations of child loss, we thought maybe a change of venue might be helpful. We started looking for a new house. Saying goodbye to the house we shared so many memories with Sawyer in seemed terribly sad, but staying brought its own challenges, so we figured we could at least look at new houses. The search proved challenging and house after house just wasn't right. I'm not sure if it was the deficiencies of the homes themselves or the emptiness in me, but I would get my hopes up after each internet query and each time I would go see the house in person, find too many flaws, and end up in tears. My poor realtor has seen me ugly cry so many times, I feel like I should offer him a larger commission, a co-pay at least in the equivalent I paid the therapist. So, we stayed in our home and just escaped as often as we could afford, emotionally and financially.

We knew early on that we were going to need counseling, so we signed up for individual counseling as well as counseling as a family. Nothing was great. We participated in a series of group counseling series that I believe helped a little. We would meet together as a family, do a remembrance activity together, and then split off into age-appropriate groups for small group counseling sessions. Sterling loved going to group sessions! Turns out friends, crafts, and snacks were enough in that time and space for her to feel validated and supported. Talking about Sawyer clearly helped give her a language to speak about death and Sawyer, so I was grateful she got something out of it. Grayson had a more difficult time, his smaller group included only two other teens, and both were girls. Jack hated it. In fact, he and another man in the group bonded over how much they hated the sessions and how they were only doing it for their family. I didn't love it, it wasn't exactly what I needed personally, but it was a box on the "healthy grieving checklist" that I could check off. "Teach a child/teen to grieve in healthy ways, go to counseling." Check. I'm grateful everyone played along and went to enough sessions to at least say we gave it a shot. It is something I anticipate we will return to throughout our lives, all of us, as different life challenges will be impacted by Sawyer's death.

I feel like I have talked a lot about things we did to cope along the way, especially in the early aftermath of Sawyer's death. But since one of the reasons I am writing this is to blow open the conversation about grief, I can't do that without sharing what helped me most in trying to cope with losing a part of me, losing my child. It's not pretty, so don't say you weren't warned. A big part of my coping strategy was to handle things that arose in my *own time* and in my *own way*. When I could do that without judgment it helped me so much in my steps towards healing. When I was judged or felt judged for the ways I handled things, and in the time I handled them, it set me back. My entire life was now about surviving and helping my children survive this terrible tragedy and it was frustrating that things people said and did had such an impact on our healing journey. Both for the good and the bad. It was another reminder that there was little I could control, so what I could, I needed to latch on to.

I read about others who took the road of alcohol and drugs to try and cope with the death of their child, but for me that wasn't a road I wanted to go down. Jack didn't either. It just seemed for those traveling that specific road it didn't really work anyway, plus we wanted to maintain spiritual commitments we had made to not engage in those forms of coping, so we didn't. But we did do a lot of grief eating. We all gained weight. Sterling subsisted on cucumbers, milk, and crackers. I pretty much let Grayson dictate the menu at our house, so it revolved around a lot of prepared foods and ordering from fast casual restaurants. We ate fast food the year after Sawyer died more times than we ever had in Grayson's entire life. Jack stopped running for the most part and as I was literally on the way to the gym to meet with a trainer for the first time when Sawyer died, I didn't go back to the gym. We knew our eating habits needed to get back under control, but we were going to let it happen in time. Coping with food, not healthy or productive, had some results in terms of immediate gratification and survival though, so we tolerated it. I was sensitive every time someone mentioned how big our children were getting. I imagine they weren't talking about the weight, but it felt like that. I wished they wouldn't comment at all. When nature finally kicked me hard enough, I knew I needed to get back to the gym but I couldn't go to the one we had been to with Sawyer, so I joined a different one, less family oriented. I was getting things for me back under control and would approach the family soon thereafter. I was coping. Until I had to cancel our old gym membership.

It was December 2017, so technically it was our second Christmas since Sawyer died. The first Christmas we were numb, so I felt like it almost didn't count because at that point it had only been two months and we were still in shock. Plus, Finn had come home from college, a welcomed distraction as it served as the brotherly interaction Sterling and Grayson needed to feel and Jack and I needed to witness. But in 2017, Finn was an ocean away in England engaged in service for our church, and of course, still and forever, no Sawyer. We had managed to muddle through Christmas 2016, I truly believe, simply on autopilot. We dissociated from the literal bells and whistles of the season and literally forced ourselves through the motions, purely for the children. Everyone outside our little family saw and labeled it as "Our First Christmas Without Sawyer." So many people went out of their way to help us feel loved. The second year, people were busy. First-responders to our grief, while still close by, had moved on and while they were saddened by our plight, they didn't know how or what they needed to do, so they did nothing. Writing it, it sounds critical. I don't mean it to be. It's just an explanation of where we were at emotionally. We were empty.

Jack got sick one night that December with a fever, literally from grief. He had been particularly worked up missing Sawyer, understandably agitated by a huge crisis at work that wasn't his fault but for which he was being blamed, and he just couldn't take the weight. He went into work late and typed this message on Facebook:

*"My body has been raging with a literal fever since last night. It's likely grief related. Most things are these days. I said prayers to God that someone would reach out to me in my time of need. It turns out that over a year later, the emotional first responders have slowed in their responses. As I dreamed, I ran into an old friend. I was hoping he could bring peace and comfort, but he could not. As I am getting ready now for work for the second half of the day, I decided that I better suck it up and get some things done. For the last fourteen months, we stopped going to the YMCA together as a family. Everything has changed and we are*

*figuring out how to navigate our new life. Until now, it has been too painful to downgrade to a single membership from a family membership. Today was the day I would suck it up. I called and just found out I have to do it in person. Fighting through tears over the phone was hard enough. Now I have to do it in person?"*

I was running errands near the gym I hadn't returned to (and wouldn't without Sawyer) when I read his post. I decided I would muster up strength and just go in and take care of it. I had been feeling stronger, so I pulled into the parking lot, parked, and gave myself a pep talk in the car. Then I walked in and told the woman at the counter what I needed to do. As she asked me to spell my last name, I started to slow my speech as I tried to fight back the tears. "Are you okay, miss?" I was wearing shades inside the building, tears streaming down my face, and a crack in my voice. "No, I am not but I will be after you take care of this for me." She completed the paperwork, had me sign the papers, and sent me on my way. She was compassionate but clearly uncomfortable. Before I left, I said to her, "My ten-year-old son died. Just over a year ago, which is why we don't come here anymore as a family. It breaks our heart just to drive by. My husband tried to take care of this membership issue over the phone and I know it's not your fault, but he was told he had to come in. I need you to communicate to your management how painful this was for me to come in and use that pain as a guide as you create policies and procedures for these types of circumstances. The public pain this caused could have been avoided." As I turned and walked out, I could hardly breathe. I ran to my car and sat in it while I cried and tried to regain composure enough to drive the twenty minutes home. Handling my grief tasks and crying profusely during and after their completion was a coping strategy I used more than once.

In response to Jack's post, one of Jack's elementary school teachers made a comment that struck me. She said, "I am sorry that more places don't operate from a standpoint of compassion and as a culture we are ill-equipped to know how to support people in their grief." She was right and we were finding how true her sentiment was over and over again as we encountered so many mundane tasks that required us to retell our tragic story in one sentence, in public, in order to take care of business. When I told a friend I needed to cancel the membership, she said, "What about all the money you have wasted already? You need to go and cancel. You could've used the money to travel or do something to honor Sawyer." Totally true. But not what I needed to hear. What I needed my friend to understand is that we lost so many things in addition to Sawyer when he died. I could write another book alone about those things, things you'd never consider unless you lived it.

The gym was another big secondary loss. Water is the great parenting equalizer, right? You can go to water anywhere and the little ones all the way up to the adults can have fun, and the rec center pool was that for our multi-aged family. Plus, the boys loved to ditch Jack and me on the treadmills and go and play basketball together. It made them feel independent. They loved to be active together and since Sawyer died, we'd all put on our grief weight, both because of our diet and because Sawyer was the one who got us all moving. We missed that about him, and we missed that for ourselves. There were the big things and the little things we lost all at once and recognizing them all took time and we still aren't done acknowledging them all. The definition of the word accept means "to consent to receive" or "to take something willingly." I cannot accept Sawyer is gone from my daily life nor can I accept all the things taken from or made too painful for me and my family because of his death. I do not accept that we lost amusement parks or grilled cheese sandwiches on the sandwich maker, but all of us are slowly starting to acknowledge them. To make such an acknowledgement all at once I believe would have killed us.

So, I imagine I will be coping with these things, big and small, until I die. Coping wasn't a matter of one day or one week or one year, and then the tasks were over and we were free to deal with Sawyer dying, free to be healed. In some ways I wish there actually was a checklist of tasks because then I could get a sense that once the list was complete, my grief could subside. Grief doesn't work in a linear way and the only rule it follows is that there are no rules for grief.

In high school Debate Team, one of the fifty-cent phrases everyone would toss around was "hasty generalizations." It was overplayed on the high school debate circuit and so I dropped it from my vocabulary as an adult. I'm bringing it back now. In grief we as a society tend to operate under hasty generalizations. "She is sad, she must not be coping well." Or even, "She isn't coping well because she's engaging in XYZ!" Conversely, we as a culture tend to believe the opposite as well. "She must be coping because she is smiling," or "She is doing well, she must be healed." When we speak in sweeping hasty generalizations, we are doing everyone a disservice. It's how racism, sexism, and all the other "-isms" get perpetuated, because we see one thing in one person and decide to apply that to everyone else in that category. Grievers are not one thing at any given time. You can be happy and crying and sad and smiling. The day-to-day tasks required me to put on certain faces, which I did most days, but often they were not an indication of how I was coping nor how I was healing.

A friend saw me at a Christmas party not soon after the YMCA experience and said, "You look well, you look *human* again. I was really worried about you. When I would see you every day at pick up, you didn't look well. But you look like a *real* person again." Actual words spoken to me. You can imagine how that made me feel. *What must I have looked like? Yeah, I wasn't well. I am not "well." Or am I? And what does that mean for me, for my family, for my grieving, for Sawyer? Does it mean I have lost the torch of my grief, thereby abandoning Sawyer? Why would you say that to me?*

Let's sidebar for a minute to talk about school pick up time. All of my experiences and memories at that particular school had been with Sawyer, since the other boys were older than elementary school and Sterling wasn't old enough for school yet when we moved into town. Now, I was going to have to pick up Sterling there every day. I met with the teacher before the start of the school year and she brought up pick up. She said, "I imagine pick up is going to be difficult for you. Can I make other arrangements for you to get Sterling so you don't have to go to the same door every day you went to for two years to grab Sawyer?" I hemmed and hawed and told her not to make a fuss, I would be fine. After further insistence on her part, I agreed, another option would be awesome, so she made it happen. The first day of school came to an end and we tried our new pick-up method and it didn't work. I told her I would suck it up and do the usual way and she again insisted she'd find another way. "I haven't had a child die but I have had terrible things happen and I know sadness and if I can help you avoid it in some small measure by making alternative plans,

I'm going to do it." And she did. I would be able to cope by changing up my routine.

Unfortunately, not everyone else was on board. After about a week of our new method, I noticed I was getting some stares by some bus drivers and staff members. It was obvious they didn't like that a parent was given "special treatment" with this new pick-up method and I am sure it didn't help that this particular parent was married to the superintendent. I mentioned it to Sterling's teacher and she said not to worry about it, she had permission and it was fine. She didn't tell every single bus driver or staff member what was happening but those in charge knew and were supportive. But each day the stares and eye rolls got worse, so I eventually caved and told the teacher I would do regular pick up. People who didn't understand the circumstances of a situation judged me and let me know of their judgment and made coping with this season of my grief journey that much more difficult. Pick up was excruciatingly painful. I cried every day for months for those few minutes, in addition to the other times of the day I cried. Plus, I had to hide it for Sterling. I didn't want her to see her sad mom at the end of each day, so I threw on a smile and gave her a hug and dried my tears under my sunglasses as we walked to the car, Sterling chattering away. Then here was the person telling me that in my coping, she thought I looked terrible. I was coping at the time the best way I could. I think she understood that, but instead of telling me at the Christmas party how proud she was of me enduring what was clearly a difficult time, she mentioned how badly I'd looked and how now I looked as though I was *accepting* Sawyer's death. Can you see why I don't like to leave the house very often or engage in small talk? Part of my coping was wearing sunglasses and just showing up. I didn't think I had a choice. Then I learned I did have a choice and some people didn't show up in their grief, they didn't put one foot in front of the other, and my doing so was a success. A success I needed to be praised for, not complimented in a way that came across as backhanded.

Counseling sort of helped, handling things in my own way and in my own time sort of helped, and surprisingly enough, Facebook also sort of helped. In the immediacy of the events surrounding Sawyer's death, I was radio silent. After his Celebration of Life was over and things were starting to sink in and I had so many thoughts and emotions I didn't know what to do with, I turned to Facebook. I was nervous about my first emotional post about Sawyer. Before this, I really kept most of my posts to the parenting antics I endured, the crazy meals I would eat, or the funny memes I'd found browsing the internet. Splaying my emotions and feelings out for the world to read wasn't really my thing (ironic now, eh?) but I didn't know what else to do. I didn't like leaving the house, I didn't really have anyone in particular to talk to, so I talked to everyone and no one at the same time through social media. People rag on social media a lot, and I hear their complaints. It is, for many, replacing real friendships and causing damage to relationships and I completely understand this complaint. For me, however, in my grief, it gave me a responsive outlet. I knew early on in Sawyer's trauma the public nature of my grief, whether I wanted it to be that way or not. I decided to embrace the lack of privacy and let the whole world know of my pain.

In the hospital, Jack and I shared so many terrible experiences, so many of which only he and I will die knowing. But there were other things people could know and I wanted them to know, in time. I told Jack in the empty hospital room that resembled the empty tomb of the Savior, "I don't know how, but we can't let this break us. We just can't." He said to me, "Jaime, we are heartbroken and will be probably forever. But we are not broken." But as time passed, this unquenchable sorrow was eating me alive and it was like a poison. I felt if I didn't get it out of me, it would kill me, and Facebook became the way I could get it out. I started using the hashtag #heartbrokenbutnotbroken as more of a reminder to myself that even though things were bleak and I was feeling broken in ways I couldn't describe, I was not broken. I am not broken. I repeated it out loud every time I typed it. Sometimes it came with a question mark after it, sometimes it was followed by an exclamation mark. As I shared more of my thoughts on Facebook, a theme began to emerge in the public and private comments. People were grateful I was willing to share my grief journey with them. People felt the humanity of grief in the words Jack and I were sharing on our social media accounts. People understood better what we were feeling and how those feelings were manifested because of our stories and memories shared. They said our posts helped them understand pain, child loss, tragedy, and grief collectively in real ways.

They were building empathy for others around them who were also grieving by reading what we had to say and by sharing our journey with them. On top of that, we also had people sharing with us they had become organ donors after reading all the things we were posting about advocating for organ donation, so that was another plus. Sharing our story in the lessons I was teaching at church, posting on social media, and relating face-to-face with people was difficult for me, but I found these endeavors ultimately gave me a strength and a release. Opening up about Sawyer and the reality of how I was feeling instead of sharing some sugar-coated version, resonated with people and gave me strength and helped me find purpose in my suffering.

One friend shared that reading about our journey helped her deal with the grief she has felt for thirty years about never being able to have a child.

*"You have really made me think. I have been mad and sad for years! What I hear you say is that paths change. Children didn't happen for us and I was mad every time I sat in church and heard about families. Every time my friends had babies and I had to be happy and throw showers, after a while I stopped going to church. It was easier. My friends got older and babies stopped coming so it was a smoldering issue until grandbabies started coming, holidays, always something. I have never accepted our path. Maybe it's time because I sure can't change it."*

We talked. She found power in the idea that it was okay that she grieved the life she always thought she would have but didn't. It was powerful to feel permission to grieve without feeling like it made her less of a disciple. It's not to say that seeing all the babies born all those years wouldn't have still made her sad. I see a little boy in our congregation who is Sawyer's age and I can't sit behind him at church anymore. The way he hugs his mom, the way his scrawny body can't hold his suit up, the cowlick in his hair. It's too hard to watch and I understand her sentiment. But I realized part of my coping was ironically found in sharing my sadness and hearing that while others hadn't suffered their child dying in front of them, they had suffered in other ways, and suffering was part of the experience of life. It's not that I wanted others to suffer so I wouldn't be alone. Of course not.

I just wanted to hear about their inevitable experiences with sadness, loss, and pain. Not the initial gut punch, not the eventual healing, but hearing about the actual ugly, day-in-day-out of what grief looks like to others, really helped me understand my own grief.

Saying Sawyer's name and hearing others say his name is still an important coping strategy. The bracelets we made with Sawyer's name on them and the SOY anagram (Be Strong, Outrageous, You) remains a lifeline for me. Seeing that people remembered Sawyer by wearing the bracelet in his honor helped give me breath each day. Seeing people honor and remember our sorrow by taking pictures wearing the bracelet doing things they needed Sawyer's strength for gave me strength. People did outrageous things and took pictures wearing the Sawyer bracelet. They travelled to exotic places and took photos wearing the bracelet. They ran marathons for the first time, sat in doctors' offices awaiting scary news, faced new challenges at new jobs, and even just lived their everyday ordinary lives all the while wearing Sawyer's bracelet, channeling his love and strength, and remembering the extraordinary life he lived. Seeing all the photos brought a sense of love and community and support and helped me cope with the loneliness I felt when Sawyer died. People sent me these photos and messages and there was a power to them all. One friend sent me this note,

*"I just wanted to tell you that I suffer with major depressive disorder and had a horrible weekend last weekend. Slept for 48 hours, cried, etc., pulled myself up and finally got to work on Tuesday afternoon. Looked at my bracelet and actually read what it said and realized what that bracelet was for me: a reminder to thank God for each day, pray for help with struggles, I am perfect just the way I am and God told me I must live every day for Sawyer and those who didn't get to live life for long. I have that opportunity and won't take it for granted. That's why I got the bracelet. To live. And not give up. And be myself. Sawyer has already done more in his short life than some people do in 90 years. Thank God for that. Just wanted to share with you. Love you and pray for you."*

Notes and photographs, some deeply meaningful, some whimsical and light, helped me deal with Sawyer's death. Every single one of them has impacted me and collectively served to be a tremendous blessing to me that ultimately did two things which helped me survive: reminded me I wasn't alone in my grief and reminded me that Sawyer would not be forgotten.

# Chapter 16

# *The Conclusion*

(I am not sure there is a conclusion to grief during this life.)

I WANTED MY LIFE, LIKE I WANT MY BOOK, TO BE THIS NICE NEAT little package. It would be filled with order and logic, tied up in beautifully thick paper with a modern and simple bow on top. Who was I kidding? If that has been your life, *you* should write a book because I think you are a modern-day miracle of your own. Seriously. From my experience, few people live that kind of life and I am no different. Life is messy. Life is chaotic. So is this book. It is messy and scattered at times, but it is my sincere hope that my mess can help even just one person understand the chaos of grief and the mind and behaviors of someone grieving. This chapter could alternatively be titled: "What I Am Learning About Grief" (I'd like to say "Learned" but it is most definitely not a finished project). But I called it "The Conclusion" because I still crave some part of that tied-up-in-a-bow version of my life.

So, here's my final list.

I've learned that sharing my story gives other people permission to acknowledge their own story.

I've learned that joy and pain can live together, and that grief and gratitude can hold the same space. Two seemingly opposing emotions can share space in your heart and your mind, words and deeds.

I've learned that loss of control feels terrible. Anything anyone can do to help you regain control is helpful and a gift.

Loss of control by us doesn't mean loss of control by God, or the Universe, or whatever you believe in. We are reminded of that through tender mercies—often in the form of others responding to impressions to act.

I've learned that words have power to hurt and as much power to heal.

I've learned that complete strangers can feel our personal pain and can help lift our burdens.

I've learned that in our darkest hours people can be there for us, if we let them in.

I've learned that in our darkest hour there are unfortunately people who are out for themselves who will selfishly make your tragedy about them. Avoid those people.

I've learned that children are resilient and that children can hold happiness and sadness in the same space as well.

Time doesn't heal everything, there is not a purpose in everything, however building a relationship with God or a higher power does qualify as an outcome, not necessarily a purpose of tragedy.

Grief is exhausting.

Grief changes you.

I've learned you don't become the perfect parent overnight, even though tragedy shines a light on the mistakes you've made and all the ways you want to improve immediately. You are still only human and there is no magic parenting pill. And we need to give each other more credit than judgment where our children are concerned.

I've learned that grief is everywhere— it doesn't just accompany death. While it is different, it is still bitter.

I've learned that our personal traumas and tragedies are just that, personal. These events and situations are often of such a personal nature that we hesitate sharing them, and rightfully so for many reasons. People can be judgmental and exposing ourselves is humbling. But until we share our experiences, let others in, and help people understand some of the implications of our grieving because of our tragedies, we will never truly be able to mourn with those who mourn and comfort those in need of comfort in ways that actually draw us closer as communities and societies.

. . . . . . . . . . . . . . . . .

So, I totaled my new car just days before the second Thanksgiving after Sawyer died. It had been new to *me* anyway, newer to the person who put the first 100,000 miles on it. It's even dumber than that. I totaled it after owning it for six weeks. Getting to the point of purchasing the car was an ordeal. When Sawyer died, I had been driving my black Honda Odyssey for years. I loved that van. We bought it fairly used but it was a big expense for us and we scrimped to make it happen. I remember being away on a girls' weekend with friends once and we were leaving a restaurant walking to my car and said out loud, "I love my car." I was always the designated driver on my girls weekends away with friends because I was the only one who didn't drink, but I didn't care because I loved my van. I drove the car another year after Sawyer's death, but it was sad. It was filled with memories and emptiness I can't explain. It came time for Sterling to start school and I was dropping her off and picking her up at "Sawyer's school," and suddenly that routine tipped the scales and the van became too much of a trigger. I would turn around to say goodbye as she hopped out of the car and be flooded with visions of Sawyer. I tried changing my routine, changing my patterns, walking her in versus letting her hop out at the drive through lane. None of it mattered. I was a sobbing mess. I knew the van would have to go.

I spent six weeks researching, test driving, and comparison shopping. I had a strict budget but I also had things I needed, mostly things I wanted. We live forty-five minutes from everything so driving to test drive or examine just one car was at least a two-hour project, so I would do as many as possible after dropping Grayson and Sterling off at school and returning in time for pickup. It was emotional and exhausting. Everyone would ask, "Are you trading in? Your van is in great condition but it's old, so I am guessing you are wanting an upgrade?" Nope, I want something entirely different. Grayson had his own attachments to the van he spent his childhood goofing off with his brothers in, so he also had a list of things he needed (wanted) from the new car. Meshing all of this with our budget became tricky, but eventually I pulled it off. Nissan Pathfinder. Check. Bought it, drove it, fell hard and fast in love with it, as did the rest of the family.

I was skeptical about making the purchase. I felt like I was betraying Sawyer's memory, abandoning him and the old car for a newer, different version of our life. It was hard even though driving a new (to me) car seems exciting and fun. Eventually I was in a good place with the car and as soon as all those emotions settled, I loved that car. I treated it ever so carefully. I was crazy about not eating in the car and not scratching the leather. I cared tenderly for this silly car. For many people this would seem like no big deal, but if you'd seen the negligent way we'd kept the van on a day-to-day basis, you'd know caring for the Pathfinder was an act of love. My B.S. in Psychology didn't get me far, but it taught me enough that clearly there was some transference going on. And in an instant, my "new" car was gone.

I had picked up Sterling from school and was driving through the village, what locals call our town square, and stopped at a two-way stop sign. I waited for the other car to make her turn, looked left, right, left, and proceeded to go straight. I heard the horns as the airbags deployed and we were suddenly spinning through the intersection. I was confused and then realized the car was smoking, or at least it smelled like it was, so I jumped out, made sure it was safe to get Sterling out, grabbed her and we waited on the side of the road. We were in town, so the driver who hit me was going slow(*ish*) and I had been at a stop sign so I barely had any time to accelerate before getting hit. Everyone was fine. Physically. After the shock of what happened wore off and I realized all the things that could've happened, I lost it. Added to that, all of the airbags on my car deployed because we took the hit directly at a "T" so the police officer was pretty sure my car was totaled. Two days later, we got a call from our insurance that indeed confirmed his suspicions. I had mostly worked through the emotions of us all being okay and then realized my car would not be. I know, I have heard it one hundred times: It's just stuff and stuff can be replaced. I understood the notion in my head, in fact I knew it better than most, but still the car had been its own ordeal for me to work through and now I was going to have to do it all over again. I cried for days every time I thought about losing the car and having to replace it. Finally, one night Jack said, "Think about it. It is the first real thing you have invested in and been excited about since Sawyer died. You loved that car. And in an instant it was gone. Sound familiar?"

Some people might think it is crazy to draw this parallel, because of course losing your child is not the same as losing your car. Let's not insult each other by thinking that's what I am saying in the slightest. What I am trying to say is, after experiencing the worst trauma in your life, nothing is just what it is anymore. There are two concepts here. The first is, on some level, when you have experienced trauma or tragedy, you redefine the way you think about things. For example, before Sawyer died, when someone would tell me something bad about their day, I would often reply, "Oh, that's terrible." No, dropping your milk jug in the parking lot is not terrible. It's a bummer, but it's not terrible. Not making the basketball team, that's extremely disappointing, but it's not terrible. Losing your child, your spouse, your house burning down, a terminal diagnosis—those things are terrible.

That said, crashing your car after losing your child isn't just crashing your car. Getting a flat tire after you've had three flat tires already in the month (true story—all nails!) isn't just another hassle. It's overwhelming. It can be debilitating. All of these experiences take an emotional tax on you, some more than others. But when you are dealing with trauma, tragedy, or sorrow, these mundane inconveniences become the tipping point in your fragile emotional state, and they can break you. This is what people don't seem to understand. "But it's just a nail in a tire." No, it's not. It's not having slept through the night for three weeks because your daughter is having Sawyer nightmares and needs help at 2 a.m., 4 a.m., and up at 6 a.m., plus your son went from straight A's to straight F's over the anniversary of your son's death, plus your son's death and all those feelings plus your flat tire. Everything good and bad that happens is wrapped up with all of these other emotions related to your grief and handling them can be challenging at best, debilitating at worst.

I got a text the other night from my friend Nicole, Isaac's mom. She texted me to say that *it* happened. Someone told her what no one ever wants to hear in their grief: "Don't you think it is time you move forward? Stop focusing on the past and move on. You need to pull it together. Stop being so sad. Life is to be lived!" It took the wind out of her and it took the wind out of me. No one has said this to me yet, but I sense it. I think those who believe this in my life keep it to themselves. The research on grief says this is bogus and I'm calling foul too! People need to heal in their own time and in their own way. This comment is the very reason I wanted to write this book. People handle sorrow in different ways, and we have to be willing to accept these differences and give others the space and assistance needed to heal.

Let me clarify the word "space." It doesn't mean abandon. It doesn't mean ignore. It doesn't mean empty. It means a location, a place for people to grieve, probably more metaphorical than literal, although I've definitely needed both. When we disappear from people's lives because others carry a weight we can't handle, or we think they should be handling better, we disregard our values related to caring for those around us. When we tell people they have been grieving long enough and put limitations on our willingness to comfort them when they need comfort, we are telling the Savior we have limits on our love, in spite of the limitless love He has shown to us. Again, we need to be willing to serve people in the way they need to be served in their grief.

Thursday, November 2017. (You might call it Thanksgiving.) We were in a stupor. It wasn't technically our first Thanksgiving without Sawyer, but the first one happened less than a month after his death, so that was a whole other thing. We wanted to get away but didn't know where to go so we just decided to pretend it was a regular long weekend and stay home to chill and do nothing. Work had been more exhausting than usual for Jack, and Grayson was still playing schoolwork catch up from being out at the one-year mark of Sawyer's death. In the end, staying home was an inspired decision because I was in the car accident three days before Thursday, which sucked time, money, and emotion out of us that we didn't even really have to give. Leaving sounded tough but staying home was feeling tough as well. Before, we'd always hosted Thanksgiving with family and friends or gone somewhere family and friends were hosting. Gatherings included games, fun, food, crowds, all of it. All of the things that after Sawyer's death, we couldn't deal with, but we missed terribly. We had several people ask us if we had plans. That was thoughtful. We had a couple people offer for us to join them in their family gatherings. That was kind. There was one family from the congregation we barely knew, but the mom asked us to join her large family gathering. I told her it would just be too much, but we appreciated the offer. I told her in passing I missed the gathering but just couldn't muster the energy to put on the façade, or worse have a public meltdown. She called me the next day and said, "What about brunch on Thursday? We could have you and your kids to play and we could have brunch before the big meal and you all can leave at your discretion." We thought about it, discussed with the family, and decided to go. Grayson wanted to opt out and we let him. We went to their home that morning and it was so mellow. She had gone out of her way to prepare the food she needed to take to her dinner the night before so she could be attentive to us and just befriend us as we ate eggs and cinnamon rolls on an otherwise gloomy Thursday. It was perfect. To me it illustrates the notion of serving people in the way they need to be served, not in the way you want to serve them.

I was relaying this experience to my sister and mother the following weekend and my sister asked some legitimate questions. "So how do you know how far to take it? Because I would feel like that was me being pushy if I asked you to come to dinner and you said no. To then ask if you wanted to come to brunch, to me, would come across as being pushy. If you'd said no to that, should she have offered to bring you breakfast? Where do you draw the line between thoughtful and overbearing?" This is the rub, right? Most of us want to be helpful and serve but we don't want to impose or come across as insistent. The thing about grief is the complications and confusion it brings. The ever-popular question, "What can I do for you?" is well intentioned but felt almost like a joke at that point. Many times in grief, the griever has no idea what they need. I've mentioned this before. Many times we didn't know what we needed, what we wanted. We couldn't find clarity of thought. So how do you know the difference between offering and imposing? This has to be the point you rely on your conscience, your God, your beliefs or whatever mix of those works for you. You know when you have gone too far or when you haven't gone far enough in your willingness to mourn and comfort. I believe exercising balance and living close to your beliefs will guide your best efforts. To everyone who inquired about our plans, that was nice. To everyone who offered us to join them, that was nice. To the one who created a space for us to celebrate and grieve simultaneously (both literally and figuratively), we will be especially grateful. Who knows, maybe next year we will host again. Maybe we will never host again. We might retreat further or we might branch out and do something we have never done before. The point is, there is no pattern and there is no end to the complications grief brings. No end in this life anyway. So be patient with those grieving and make no judgments, hold no expectations, and recognize that the only Thanksgiving or holiday or gathering they want is the final one that reunites them with their loved one and vanquishes their sorrow. Until then, don't run away from the challenge of loving a griever.

We also have to realize what healing looks like is different for everyone. All the workbooks and textbooks and stories and brochures and pamphlets and feel-good articles that talk about grief say essentially the same thing: there is no avoiding grief. You can't go over it or around it, the only way is through the grief. Through it. I don't know how I am going to get through it.

Jack has always told the kids to hold their breath every time we drive and pass through a tunnel. Sometimes the tunnels are too long and the kids get exasperated and give up at different times, but they all give up because they can't hold their breath long enough. Every time I read the only way to heal from the grief is to travel through it, I think of those long tunnels. I think of the one on the way to Virginia Beach. The one none of us could ever successfully master passing through breathless on our many sojourns to the waves. I sometimes think to myself, my life is now this long tunnel and I am never going to heal because I cannot make it through and there is no way around it. It is just too long.

It was during my time of reading so much about grief and healing and sorrow and wellness, I was reminded of the Japanese philosophy of Kintsugi. Translated from Japanese it means "golden joinery" or "golden repair." I had read about this in a fictional novel years prior but had forgotten about this Japanese notion. It's this idea that when something breaks and is repaired, the repair is what makes the piece individual and adds beauty and character. Maybe because I have often had times in my life, nothing to this extent, where I have felt a little cracked or felt my imperfections shining through, thus the appeal. At this time in my life, I like the idea even more. I want to heal; I want to be healed. Jeffrey R. Holland, an American educator and religious leader said, "Broken minds can be healed just the way broken bones and broken hearts are healed. While God is at work making those repairs, the rest of us can help by being merciful, nonjudgmental, and kind." I like the idea that God is working to repair my heart and my mind. His words were important to me. I feel like it takes some of the burden off of me, because I feel the weight of the burden, and—like the long tunnel—I fear it is a job too enormous to undertake myself. I also like the idea that it requires others to do a little work too, to be merciful, nonjudgmental, and kind. So, when I am crying in the hallway as the Cub Scouts walk by, don't pretend you don't see me. When I order pizza more often than I make chicken cordon bleu, don't comment on how much weight my other son is putting on. When you know I need a little friendship, but we aren't quite besties yet, introduce yourself to me, hand me a tissue, and tell me it's okay to take the time I need and occupy the space required to feel the fullness of my grief, even if it makes others uncomfortable.

I will never be the same person I was before Sawyer died. This ancient practice of fixing broken pottery was how I wanted to see my life. Instead of trashing a piece of pottery when it breaks, having it repaired with a special lacquer dusted with gold to highlight the breaks gives the previously broken piece value and uniqueness. The beautiful golden seams highlight the breaks instead of hiding them with super glue, like we all used to do as kids when repairing a broken vase after a foolish night with a babysitter and a football. "Kintsugi often makes the repaired piece even more beautiful than the original, revitalizing it with new life." Part of the reason I love this concept is precisely because it highlights the breaks, it calls the breaks out of the shadows. My soul is being repaired daily. But to pretend I will be the same person as before is unrealistic. But maybe the Japanese have it right, maybe looking the same as before isn't where the beauty lies. The beauty lies in the cracks, in the repairs.

· · · · · · · · · · · · · · · · · ·

It's funny, mourning. Some days I want to be totally alone. Some days all I want is to be surrounded by people who knew Sawyer and who speak his name freely. There is no telling what type of day it is going to be until I am in the thick of it. The inconsistency of mourning makes it terribly difficult for those who are trying to help you mourn. It is hard to teach, let alone study "How to be a Good Mourner." (Okay, technically there is a *Grieving for Dummies* book, I looked, it exists. I guess it is better than nothing?) To me, the most important way people can support mourners is by developing and exercising empathy. You cannot exercise empathy if you don't have it and that is why I am sharing the private moments of my life with anyone who wants to read it. To try and build a community of empathetic mourners in the hopes that those suffering and needing an army to support them, will have one.

I am also suggesting we need to learn and understand grief in more complex ways. The days of hearing bad news, dropping off a casserole, and moving on are past. Our discipleship requires more of us. We need to be more willing to surround ourselves in the grief of others instead of running away in fear because others' burdens are too heavy for us. We need to stop saying, "I don't want to intrude," "It isn't my place," "I don't want to bring it up or make it worse by mentioning it." All of those sentiments are excuses to avoid grief and the sadness it brings to us. It boils down to fear and selfishness and we need to overcome both of those to become better people. Christ Himself was "a man acquainted with sorrow." He wept with the family of Lazarus and He knew the outcome. He knew that holding space for sorrow and grief with those who are mourning was not showing weakness or faithlessness but quite the opposite. He knew the power of sitting one on one with those He loved and mourning with them instead of blowing over the discomfort and sadness. He would bring communion and camaraderie and would establish relationships and strengthen human ties. He knew the power of charity. When we understand the power of charity and the impact it can have on others, when we understand we must serve people in the ways they need to be served, not in the ways we want to serve them, we grow our relationships with those around us and deepen our relationship with God. Grief is an intimate emotion and sharing that with someone, helping them bear that cross, brings a level of fellowship and godliness to the relationship.

Also, in my reading and studying the thoughts and writings of other grievers, many talk about sorrow "settling into their bones." It's the idea that life does go on and is to be lived. I believe this wholeheartedly. We are *heartbroken, but not broken*. I carry Sawyer in my heart and I want to give him a wild ride. My boy was outrageous, unique, strong, kind, loving, and energetic. I want to take his memory and zest for life and live for him as much as for me. Yes, I believe his spirit lives on. This doesn't change how much I miss him every day. This doesn't change the ache in my soul as I watch his friends have birthdays and live and experience things he will never get to experience. This doesn't negate my sense of emptiness in the places Sawyer should be. It doesn't always abate the tears. It doesn't always cure my sadness. The sorrow is settling in my bones. I believe our spirits will be reunited someday. I also believe I have important work to do here, children here I need to care for and teach and grow, and I can't do that if I am buried in my grief. That is the task of Jack and me together with Finn, Grayson, and Sterling: unburying ourselves from our grief. Some weeks the work results in visible progress. Other times there are weeks where it might look like nothing has been done. Recognizing the baby steps alongside the monumental breakthroughs is important for me to do, as well as for all those who interact with me. In this progress, I would be doing a disservice to my family, to love, to life, to Sawyer's memory and to the true meaning of enduring to the end if I just abandoned my sorrow and said, "All is well." All *will* be well. I will *endure* to the end. I will *find* joy. *Peace* will accompany me in my journey. And a piece of me will *mourn*, until that final glorious day.

And until that glorious day, I hope people will be understanding and gentle with my broken heart.

**The end.**

# *Afterword*

I had a dream. It was the day after what would have been his 13th birthday, on Super Bowl Sunday, no less—he would have been stoked. (Until after the game, I heard it was a snoozer.) I haven't had many dreams about Sawyer, this one was my third. The first one was vivid but very brief. Part of my anxiety in coping with Sawyer's death is trying to find understanding that wherever he is, in whatever form, that Sawyer's spirit is happy. I yearned for this knowledge, for some peace of mind feeling that he was happy. I personally believe those who die go to a place where they will know joy and peace. Translating specific doctrine to Sawyer was where I struggled. I had received many blessings of comfort that referred to Sawyer as being safe, but I had never heard anyone use the word happy. It bothered me so much. It was my word, why was I getting hung on it? It was implied. Was it? I didn't feel settled about it. And then I had that first dream. It almost wasn't even a dream. It wasn't a vision or anything. It was a moment of clarity. I truly believe it was a moment, a flash, a few seconds God gave me as a glimpse of the other side. It happened the night after a man we went to church with had passed away. David was a young dad with a wife and four children. In my dream I saw Sawyer. And David. They were together. In white. Bright white, radically white light radiated around them. Sawyer was sitting, David was standing. They were smiling huge smiles, almost laughing. They emanated joy. I woke up in tears, but for once they felt like tears of comfort. The second one I don't remember and didn't write down because there wasn't anything I could recollect, except waking up in tears, feeling he had been a passing character in the story line that evening. But the night in February 2019, the dream was again vivid.

It started, as most dreams do, in the middle of the plot. He was with me, by my side at some sort of lecture or presentation. Lots of children were around. He was sitting next to me and I could actually touch him, I could feel him clearly. I knew he was by my side and somehow he was just back in our lives, he wasn't dead. He was alive and we all had just accepted his re-entry. There hadn't been a parade or party to usher in his return, nor did we question it, he had just assimilated back into the Six Family like he'd never been gone. He and Grayson left my side and went into the gym next door. I could hear them laughing. There was a crowd and Grayson had gently pushed their way to the front, like he was standing up for Sawyer as a sort of bodyguard. Too crowded to see whatever was happening, Grayson even hoisted Sawyer onto his shoulders and helped him climb onto the top of one of those temporary wall partitions. They both looked at me. Sawyer grinned his sneaky grin, flashed his eyes at me like he knew he could when he was trying to get away with something, which he was regularly. His eyes were saying "I know this is wrong but I'm doing it anyway."

I quietly took my index and middle fingers and did a swift mom motion for him to get down and reluctantly, but obediently, Grayson helped him get down. They went back into the gym and when they returned to me, Sawyer sat on my left leg, too big to fit into my lap. He was big, but I squeezed him and we touched our heads together. Jack was sitting on my right side and I asked him to take a picture of us, to which Jack replied, "Of course."

He took the picture and when he showed me his phone to see the photo, Sawyer wasn't in it, but I was smiling and gesturing as though he were there. It didn't make sense. Sawyer was there, right then, he was there still. I saw him with my own eyes. I felt the bridge of his nose scrunched up. I touched it with my own two hands. He even said to me, "I was born with a face that looks like I'm standing in the rain" and he squinted his eyes and looked up at the sky, crinkling his little nose, like when you are in a rainstorm. I touched his nose, I felt the wrinkles in his skin. Jack took another picture of the boys, now they were outside somehow. The photo was of Grayson tilling the garden and Sawyer helping him, but when I looked at that picture, he wasn't in the photo again. But we all accepted that he was there, we talked to him, we referenced him, he was there but somehow he was not showing up in the photographs. The dream ended.

I woke up. I was crying a slow but steady cry and as soon as I was conscious, the thought was placed into my mind, *"Could he really be this close? Could he really be this close?"* The thought wasn't my thought. I was too unaware, too confused. I was gifted this thought. He really could be this close.

The crying then turned to sobbing. I couldn't stop sobbing. For what seemed like a while, but was in actuality probably just seconds if I could assess it in real-time, I knew exactly what it felt like to have Sawyer back in my presence again. It was perfect. I felt whole. And then I was awake and felt broken again and I couldn't stop sobbing. I kept sobbing except my sobbing turned into borderline hysteria. I instinctively did the silent scream parents do when they can't actually scream because the whole house is asleep. There is suburban life that at 3 a.m. is quiet and cluttered by worry and sorrow so, wanting to lash out like a banshee in the streets and proclaim my sadness, I instead just pulled my hair and silently screamed, mouth open, no sound escaping. I was reminded what it felt like to have Sawyer back and it was perfection. Waking up to remember he was gone was torture. I tried pulling myself back into the dream, remembering every second of the dream, every touch, every color. Jack was wearing a yellow linen shirt like the ones the boys wore Easter 2012 at the Maple's house near the beach. Sawyer was wearing an Under Armor shirt and sports shorts. Grayson was younger, the age Sawyer was when he died. I know because Grayson had long locks in his hair and the brothers were close to the same height. Grayson was also wearing athletic shorts, a practice he had abandoned since entering tenth grade. Sterling and Finn weren't in the frame of the dream but they were close by, I felt it, I felt complete. It was like they were in the next room, so while I couldn't see them, I felt them. All of them, all of my family. The tears stopped momentarily as I was living in the memory of the dream again. But the tears would start again as I would jump back and forth between reality and recollection, between the sobbing and the visualizing, trying to memorize and experience each tiny segment of the dream again. Again, the thought pressing on my mind, *"Could he really be this close?"*

I reached for the stuffed lion I slept with every night. The lions were given to every member of our family by the hospice nurse while we were in the hospital with Sawyer. The raggedy animal wasn't Sawyer. It didn't feel like him. His lanky bones, his long arms, his skinny little back that meant I could touch every bone of his rib cage. I tried to make it work, but the substitute wasn't cutting it. Sawyer wasn't suddenly back in our lives, he was still gone. I was reminded of that cold fact in a very visceral way again on that night. Of course, the ache of him being gone looms in my every waking moment, but the excruciating pain of it has started to dull. Much like, as people said, it would. But that night I was reminded of that pain that cuts to the bone. It was almost like instinctively my body had to know again the guttural ache of his absence, but it also, through my dream, had to remind me what I am still living for. I am living, in part, to be able to see Sawyer again and feel wholeness, the sweet contentment of everything being right in the world, because my family is together forever. Even if only for a few mere seconds. *Could he really be that close?*

I knew I had to write it all down so I could recall every detail later, when I could see it from a better perspective. A clearer perspective. In my scattered state, I jotted it down in a note on my iPad. I could remember it all because I had just lived it. There wasn't much because again, it was only snippets of a dream. Oh yeah. And there was someone famous in the dream who was speaking at the vague event we were attending. She reminded me specifically of how important it was to not try cocaine, and of how addictive and deadly it could be. Because, it was after all, a dream, and crazy things like that interrupt the most tender of moments in dreams.

I laid in the bed and tried to stay in the space of the dream yet again, trying to re-experience each detail of the dream. The recollection would bring me to sobs again and I could calm myself back down, each time realizing more and more, I was losing the gift of the dream, by trying to experience it again because it was just upsetting me. In the dream I was happy, whole. Reliving it made me more and more upset. Yes, I do think I needed that jolt of pain, but equally I think the purpose of the dream was to give me a few seconds of pure joy. I knew I needed to focus on how I felt being with Sawyer and channel that sense, instead of channeling the exact details. Those were too sad to relive, they brought the immediate longing right back. I knew I needed to refocus my vision, but boy, that's tough. I repeated the cycle a few more times until I had a little more composure each time. Because as any parent who has lost a child will tell you, you will take any sad moment with your child over no moment at all.

The dream got me thinking back to my friend Sharon who I mentioned earlier. Remember her son Steven died over thirty years ago. He was in a car crash that took his life. Soon after Sawyer died, when I was finally taking visitors, she drove three hours to talk to me. She had asked on the phone what she could bring me and for some reason I said cake. I'm not even really a cake person (unless you are talking about the change-your-life salted caramel cake at Shyndigz in Richmond), but "cake" just came out of my mouth. When she arrived, she told me she'd had an experience making the cake. She said while she was baking it, for a brief second, she saw Sawyer in her kitchen. She'd known Sawyer from church during our time in Radford. She said, "He was there, Jaime. I saw him in my kitchen. I could see his wispy light blonde hair and that cheeky grin with his teeth. He said to me, very pointedly as I was making the cake, 'Make it a big one.' Then he was gone."

At the time I didn't know what to think. I asked her more about the moment. I asked her why she could see and feel Sawyer and I couldn't. I hadn't. People said I would, but I didn't. It made me feel terrible. If I believed all this stuff about an afterlife, which theoretically meant Sawyer could somehow show himself to me in some way, why was I unable to channel his presence? I felt inadequate. Then I remembered Sharon's theory, that perhaps he had tried to visit, but it was too hard for me to have him around and Sawyer didn't want that for me. I was not ready for him to be in my presence quite yet in this way because the pain of his physical absence was too raw. She also suggested he was maybe protecting me, because I had too much to bear and his spirit being too close was making my sensitive broken spirit too sad. So, he would watch and protect and visit others and do other things, whatever spirits do (my other kids hope it is to control oceans and learn to make fire with your fingers, but alas . . .), until the time he could be close to me again and it wouldn't keep breaking me. Who knows, but somehow that notion of him protecting me, comforted me.

As I sat in the space of my dream and the eventual calm quiet that settled back over my room, I thought about Sharon and her theory. Maybe the brokenness really was starting to leave and the heartbroken part of me was settling in better than I had realized. Maybe he really could be that close, and maybe I was starting to attune myself to him. I don't know how that translates in scientific terms. I don't know if that means the atoms of his spirit were physically occupying the same space as I was in. I don't know if that means my heart was starting to accept his death in a way I hadn't before. Maybe it meant that my heart was finally letting me carry some of the acceptance of his death alongside the new relationship I would be required to establish with Sawyer. A relationship that would have to bridge my life and his death by way of memories and hope and presence of mind. Maybe it was the beginning of my heart and brain reconciling that the only ride Sawyer would take from here on out was in my heart, so I needed to take him on a wild ride. I don't know. I may never know.

The day after my dream, I went to dinner with Nicole. It was a habit we had continued every couple of months after our boys died. Those dinners offer a safe space to say the things no one else understands or wants to hear. She talked about "graduating" from her grief counseling. She expressed a sentiment similar to the one I had felt trying to process my dream and acknowledgement of the feeling that some of the brokenness was starting to change. I told her it felt like people were always telling me to cheer up, the sun would shine, the world would be bright and happy again if I would only let it. I saw some meme that said "life is 10% what happens to you and 90% how you respond." I want to write a dissertation on the flaws I see in that notion, but anyway, the concepts are similar: buck up. Put a smile on. It's time to move on. As I spoke to her, I voiced a curiosity. I wondered if Sawyer's death was more like a cloud that casts a shadow on my life and occasionally brings in major thunderstorms, sometimes a trickle, and sometimes the smallest of shadows. Transforming my brokenness to heartbrokenness does not mean running from the cloud. The old cliché about dancing in the rain, not waiting for the sun to shine. It felt so cheesy, it almost hurt. But it quietly resonated with us both as we nodded. Some people live in the sun, some people live in the rain. Both can find a version of happiness and learn to live with the rest. I presume I will spend the rest of my life trying to figure it all out and find peace of mind and peace of heart. That is, until my ultimate peace comes when Sawyer is eternally reunited with me and our family.

A note about my family. I was blessed to have a supportive family. Not every instance of love and service they rendered was talked about in these parts of the story I have shared with you. A large part of that is due to the sacredness of the times we shared in those dark days. My family, my extended family, my husband's family whom I consider to be my family, all of them had to mourn the death of Sawyer. They also lost the relationships they had with the "before" versions of us all. I hate that for them as I hate it for our immediate family. And while not everyone was mentioned on paper, they all hold a special place in my heart for the way they came and mourned with us.

I am also blessed to feel the grace of those who know the depth of my pain in losing a child because they carry it too and share it with me. I will be forever grateful for their friendship, in spite of the cost: the Stauffers, the Klines, the Guthries, the Gregorys, the Bodnariks, Sharon McAllister, Kathleen Doyle, Laura Floyd, and Karen Guye.

# Works Cited

Angelou, Maya., Boyers, Sara Jane Basquiat, Jean Michel. *Life Doesn't Frighten Me: Poem*. New York : Stewart, Tabori & Chang, 1993. Print.

Arendt, Hannah. *The Human Condition*. University of Chicago Press, 1958.

Bednar, David A. "The Tender Mercies of the Lord." April 2005. www.lds.org/general-conference/2005/04/the-tender-mercies-of-the-lord?lang=eng.

Blixen, Karen (Isak Dineson). Quote on page 7 from an interview with Bent Mohn in *The New York Times Book Review* (November 3, 1957), later quoted by Hannah Arendt in *The Human Condition* (1958).

Book of Mormon, The. Trans. Joseph Smith, Jr. Salt Lake City, UT: The Church of Jesus Christ of Latter-day Saints, 1981, Mosiah 18:9.

Bowen, Shayne M. "Because I Live, Ye Shall Live Also." October 2012. https://www.lds.org/general-conference/2012/10/because-i-live-ye-shall-live-also?lang=eng

Couric, Katie. "Katie Couric on Surviving Christmas After Her Husband Passed." *Time*, Nov. 30, 2017, time.com/5040988/katie-couric-husband-holidays/.

Clemmer, Jaime. "Heartbroken, But Not Broken," Growing Up in the Valley, November 2017. *Issuu*, https://issuu.com/growingupinthevalley/docs/november_2017_issuu.

Haley, Eleanor. "What Does it Mean to Be Strong in Grief?" in *what's your grief?* May 21, 2020. https://whatsyourgrief.com/what-does-it-mean-to-be-strong-in-grief/.

Hamilton, Robert Browning. "Along the Road." *The Best-Loved Poems of the American People*. Reissue edition, sel. Hazel Felleman. New York: Doubleday, 1936, 537.

Holland, Jeffrey R. "Like a Broken Vessel." October 2013. www.lds.org/general-conference/2013/10/like-a-broken-vessel?lang=eng.

Holland, Henry Scott. "Death is Nothing at All," *Family Friend Poems*, www.familyfriendpoems.com/poet/henry-scottholland/.

Marriott. Neill F. "Abiding in God and Repairing the Breach." October 2017. https://www.churchofjesuschrist.org/study/general-conference/2017/10/abiding-in-god-and-repairing-the-breach?lang=eng.

Richardson, Jan. "Blessing for the Brokenhearted" © Jan Richardson from *The Cure for Sorrow: A Book of Blessings for Times of Grief*. Orlando, FL: Wanton Gospeller Press. janrichardson.com.

Richman-Abdou, Kelly. "Kintsugi: The Centuries-Old Art of Repairing Broken Pottery with Gold." *My Modern Met*. September 5, 2019. https://mymodernmet.com/kintsugi-kintsukuroi/.

Shakespeare, William. *Macbeth by William Shakespeare*. Global Media, 2007.

Suhan, Christine. "No, Everything Does Not Happen for a Reason." *To Save A Life*, 6 Feb. 2018, tosavealife.com/relationships/everything-not-happen-reason/.

Thoreau, Henry David. Journal 1: 1837–1844, ed. Elizabeth Hall Witherell et al. Princeton: Princeton University Press, 66.

Uchtdorf, Dieter F. "Come, Join with Us," October 2013. Come, www.churchofjesuschrist.org/study/general-conference/2013/10/come-join-with-us?lang=eng

Uchtdorf, Dieter F. "Fourth Floor, Last Door." October 2016. www.lds.org/general-conference/2016/10/fourth-floor-last-door?lang=eng.

Vanzant, Iyanla. See https://quotefancy.com/quote/833602/Iyanla-Vanzant-It-s-important-that-we-share-our-experiences-with-other-people-Your-story. Accessed March 17, 2021.

# About the Author

. . . . . . . . . . . . . . . . . .

Photo by Khand Tenny

JAIME CLEMMER HAS WORKED THROUGHOUT HER LIFE FOR AGENCIES whose primary focus addresses domestic and sexual violence issues. She was a strong advocate for organ donation long before Sawyer died, and still is.

Jaime graduated from BYU with a BS in psychology and a minor in women's studies. She and her husband, Jack, have four children, three of whom are living. She started the *heartbroken, but not broken* community after the death of her son, Sawyer, to acknowledge grief and honor resilience.

Jaime and her family enjoy one upping each other on game nights, eating delicious meals, and sharing their home, "Eunice," with anyone who will come visit. Yes, their house is named "Eunice." That is another story.